GW00750270

THE POWER OF
LETTING GO

BETA VERSION 2.0

JOHN PURKISS

The rights of John Purkiss to be identified as the Author of this work have been asserted by him in accordance with the Copyright, Designs and Patents Act 1988.

All rights reserved. No part of this publication may be reproduced, stored in a retrieval system or transmitted in any form or by any means, electrical, mechanical, photocopying, recording or otherwise without the prior written permission of the Author.

The information contained in this book is intended to provide helpful and informative material on the subject addressed. It is not intended to serve as a substitute for professional advice. Any use of the information in this book is at the reader's discretion. The author specifically disclaims any and all liability arising directly or indirectly from the use or application of any information contained in this book.

© 2017 John Purkiss

ISBN: 978-1-5272009-4-4

Cover Design: Jim Shannon
Layout: Susanne Worsfold
Printed and bound in Great Britain by Bell & Bain Ltd, Glasgow

For the Magician in all of us

Table of Contents

Here's your personal copy of *The Power of Letting Go*.
It's a pilot edition (or 'beta version' as they say in software).
I hope you enjoy it.

You'll notice that there are a few places where I've written
"Insert other people's examples" or "Insert other people's
experiences". If you read something that strikes a chord,
I'll be keen to hear about it.

I also want to make sure the exercises work well for both
readers and workshop participants. All feedback welcome!

Many thanks for your help.

Disclaimer

The information contained in this book is provided for general purposes only. It is not intended and should not be relied upon as medical advice. The publisher and author are not responsible for any specific health needs that may require medical supervision. If you have underlying health problems, including mental health problems, or have any doubts about the material contained in this book, you should contact a qualified medical professional.

Introduction

Most of us have something we want to happen. So you may be expecting me to say that you should take control and leap into action. No. I'm telling you to do the opposite. I'm telling you to let go.

You may find this shocking at first. Your mind may resist, but it works. People have been letting go for thousands of years. I will show you how to make it work for you.

What's your starting point?

Do any of the following descriptions sound like you?

- You're doing well but you know you could do even better. You know you're capable of so much more. Now you want to do things on a bigger scale.
- You're aware of changes in technology, the economy and politics. You want to stay ahead of the game.
- You've done a fair amount of work on yourself. Maybe you do some meditation or yoga. You see the value in letting go and might want to extend it to other areas of your life.
- You're curious. You've heard about letting go, and want to know how it works in practice.
- You have the external trappings of success, but you still feel anxious, envious or regretful. You wonder what you can do to feel better about yourself.
- Everything has gone to plan – more or less. You've got what you wanted, but you aren't happy. (Maybe you're creating drama or stress in order to feel 'alive'.)
- You meditate regularly, but feel stuck. Your life isn't moving forwards. You're wondering what to do. Should you push forwards or hold back?

- The situation looks hopeless. <u>Nothing</u> in your life is working. (I was one of those.)

The usual reason things don't happen is that something is in the way. The solution is to remove the blockage and create space. Then things start happening. Here's the process in a nutshell:

It isn't always easy to identify what's getting in the way. It could be as subtle as a mental habit that you haven't noticed. It could be a strong emotion about something in the past. Whatever it is, this book will help you to identify and let go of it.

If you don't know what you want, that's fine too. Things will become clearer as we go along.

What life is like after letting go

Whatever your starting point may be, letting go makes life much better. The more you let go, the more you'll find that:

- You feel relaxed and forget to worry.
- Things happen far more easily.
- You take the right action at the right time.
- There's little or no stress.
- Your health improves.
- Relationships are easy.
- You understand intuitively what's going on around you.
- Creativity becomes a natural part of life.
- You watch things fall into place.
- Earning money is no longer the main aim, but it happens more easily.
- You're no longer bored. Life is exciting again.
- You allow other people to be as they are.
- You laugh more.

When we let go we no longer struggle to make things happen. We give up the fight. Things happen smoothly while we relax and do whatever's appropriate. (Sometimes there may be lots of action. At other times there may be none.) We feel happy – sometimes blissful – while life unfolds around us.

Letting go doesn't mean you give up or don't care any more

- Letting go *is not* the same as giving up. More may happen rather than less. The same mental or physical effort produces bigger results.
- You may find yourself taking *more* action than before, but it will be pleasurable rather than stressful.
- Letting go *does not* mean that you don't care. In fact, you're likely to care *far more* about other people. You may also find yourself being kinder to animals.

Letting go can occur in several ways

For example:

- You become aware of some mental habit which has been running your life and causing you to suffer. You realise how absurd it is, so you drop it.
- You suffer from painful memories or anxiety. You pay attention to the pain and *feel* it. In due course it dies down and may even disappear.

Everything that works involves letting go

This book has its roots in the major spiritual traditions, which go back thousands of years. I've spent over 20 years exploring them. I've attended retreats, learned several types of meditation and tried a wide variety of other practices. Some had an effect. Some didn't. After a while I realised that everything that works involves letting go. Then I began teaching other people, who have enjoyed similar results.

You can learn and apply the material in this book in a couple of weeks. Please note that you won't need to change your religion, or any views you may hold *about* religion. This is for everyone.

There's no point waiting for science to confirm what we can experience directly

I studied economics at Cambridge University, worked in banking and management consultancy, and did my MBA at INSEAD[1]. Economics uses the scientific method, which involves observing what's going on and then formulating a theory to explain it. Sometimes a theory becomes a hypothesis which scientists can test to see if they can disprove it[2]. In due course, old theories are superseded by new ones which describe reality better. Physics is a prominent example of this process.

Knowledge acquired in this way is *objective*. It's based on objects and events in the world which – in principle – anyone can observe. By contrast, *subjective* knowledge is based on the observer's direct, personal experience. Both approaches are *empirical* to the extent that they're based on observation and experimentation.

Unsurprisingly, in some cases subjective knowledge is way ahead of objective knowledge. We can gather direct experience much faster than it can be tested scientifically. For example, people have been meditating for thousands of years, experiencing a wide range of benefits. Only recently have scientists begun to understand what happens during meditation to produce those benefits. There's a very long way to go. My point is that…

The exercises in this book will help you make your own discoveries

You and I are likely to be dead by the time science fully explains all the phenomena described in this book. So let's just give it a go and see what happens.

Some of the exercises require a few minutes of dedicated time. Others you can practise in the midst of whatever else you're doing. They've worked for large numbers of people. However, not every exercise works for everyone. Try each exercise for yourself as you read the book. In some cases you may notice a difference – or learn something – right away. In other cases, nothing may happen, at least initially. I suggest you move on and come back to it later. An exercise that gives you no insights the first time you try it may prove very useful later.

If you do the exercises thoroughly, you will develop new skills that will make you more effective at whatever you choose to do.

Allow new things to happen
Think of a time when you created space – or a space was created for you – which allowed something new to happen. Here are some examples to jog your memory:

- A relationship ended. Then someone new came along.
- A job or business ended. Then a new opportunity appeared.
- While you were too ill to do anything, something new began to take shape in your life.
- Someone cancelled an appointment, creating a space in your diary. Then something else happened.
- Your travel plans were disrupted, so you went elsewhere and had a memorable experience.
- You were meditating, running or taking a shower. Suddenly an idea came to you.

At times you may feel uncomfortable when a space appears. You may feel tempted to fill it with:

- Shopping
- Reading
- Endless tea, coffee or alcohol
- Travel
- Routine tasks
- Mundane conversations
- Watching TV or surfing the internet.

If you have a habit of filling up space, I encourage you to break it. If you relax and let go instead, you'll allow something new to happen. I will help you do this.

The complete solution is to let go completely

Most of us have grown up with the idea that, if we want something to happen, we need to focus on what we want, make plans, take action and so on. By this stage in your life, you may have noticed that it frequently doesn't work. Or it works in a way, with very painful side-effects - particularly in terms of your health and relationships. Sometimes we suffer financially too. None of this is necessary.

So what's the alternative? This book will show you - step by step - how to let go of everything, including what you want. Doing this creates the maximum amount of space and allows things to happen much more easily.

This is a huge change for most people, and it may feel scary. That's why I'm going to guide you through the process one step at a time. It will also be fun. You'll discover some surprising things about yourself. When we let go completely our lives are transformed. We're more fulfilled than ever before - with less stress.

Let's get started.

1
What do you want?

Think about what you want. It could be one or more of the following:
- Peace of mind
- A relationship
- Better relationships
- A job
- A promotion at work
- A better job
- Your own business
- A more successful business
- More money
- To create or invent something
- To do something that will change the world

What would you like less of? Here are some suggestions:
- Stress
- Frustration
- Disappointment
- Confusion
- Boredom

Or it might be something that isn't listed above. What's the most pressing thing in your life? What drives you crazy? What chews up your mental energy? What are you most excited about?

Whatever it is, please write it down in a notebook or on a sheet of paper. Now.

Please note that nothing you write is cast in stone. It's just to help you get started.

2
Start Letting Go of Your Stories

We all have stories. We tell them to ourselves and we live by them.

Stories are useful up to a point. I wrote about them in my last book, *Brand You¹*. If someone asks you what you do, it helps if you can give them a snappy answer before they get distracted. If I don't know the person, I usually say something simple such as "I'm a headhunter and I write books". Or maybe something a bit specific like "I'm recruiting a chief executive and completing a book". Then we talk about whatever interests them.

Most of us need a basic story so we can interact with people and function in society. It's like wearing clothes. Walking around naked doesn't work so well. But it also doesn't help if we become obsessed by our clothes or our stories. There's no need to keep talking about them or allow them to take over our lives.

We've assembled our stories over many years, with the help of our parents, teachers, friends, colleagues and the media. Some stories are positive, but let's start with the negative ones:

- I keep having problems with…
- I may seem to have everything but I'm still unhappy
- I don't want to show off
- People like me don't do that sort of thing
- I used to be successful, but not any more
- I'm unlucky in love
- I've got writer's block
- I'm a victim of …
- Nothing seems to work

- I'm an outsider
- I'm too old
- I'm too young
- I'm not good enough
- I feel like a loser
- I can't ...

Do you have any stories like these?

Some people are so immersed that they believe they *are* their stories. They're trapped like characters in a play. Their lives are limited by their stories.

These are *your* stories, so *you* can let them go

You may have several stories, on various topics. It's best if you work on one of them to begin with. Then you can handle your other stories in the same way.

You may have noticed that I keep referring to these stories as *yours*. Wherever they came from, it's *you* that chooses to hold onto them – or let them go. This book will help you do the latter. Simply becoming aware *that you have a story* can be very helpful.

One day my friend Jacq was driving me to the station when I asked her a question. Here's the essence of our conversation:

What's happening with you?

> All good except for business. I work hard and I'm always busy, but somehow I'm not making the sort of money I want. It's like there's a glass ceiling on it.

4

That sounds like a story to me :) What are the beliefs behind it?

> I'm not sure what you mean

What's the story you tell yourself about you and success?

> Mmm.. Well, when I look at the world the thing that pains me most is the inequality I see. Everything from access to food, money, health, joy and even sporting ability.

(She started laughing.)

> And if I'm too successful then I guess I'll become one of the perpetrators, one of the baddies creating inequality.

And what do you get out of continuing to tell yourself that story?

> If *I* can't get what I want either, then I can continue to think of myself as one of the 'good guys', rather than one of the baddies. Oh dear...

What would happen if you let go of the belief that you can't get what you want?

> That would spoil my whole story.

(Laughing at herself.)

> This is hilarious, I'm clear about my values around justice and equality but I had no idea I was holding onto a story that was holding me back. I'm so glad I've got this one out in the open. It's ridiculous.

What would be the benefit of letting go of this story now?

> Well, I'd probably find life easier to navigate and be more financially successful. Then I'd be able to contribute more money to charities that provide famine relief and medicine. And if I'm less angst-ridden perhaps I'll even have more time and energy to help address other injustices. It's a no-brainer really. I could have been stuck for the rest of my life.

Some of our stories melt away as soon as we look at them closely. Embarrassment and laughter are both helpful.

18 months later, Jacq's life had changed:

> It's amazing. Life is easier in every way, including relationships at home and at work. My business has more than doubled in size. I'm able to give more work to other people and give more money to my favourite charities.

> Now that life is easier, I'm helping in the scouting community and looking for ways of doing more elsewhere. There don't seem to be any limits to what I can do now.

Letting go of your story will create space for something new to happen.

Stories are usually based on painful experiences and/or negative beliefs. We may push them to the back of our minds in the hope that they will go away, but they don't. As the psychologist Carl Jung[2] put it, "Until you make the unconscious conscious, it will direct your life and you will call it fate."

Now it's your turn.

Turn to a blank page, pick a story to work on, and <u>write down</u> the answers to the following questions:

What's the story you tell about yourself?

What are the beliefs that underlie your story?

What short-term pleasure do you derive from holding onto each belief?

What's the pay-off from telling this story?

What's this story costing you?

What will be the benefit to you from changing now?

As I mentioned just now, you may have several stories, in which case I recommend you do this exercise several times, to identify and disentangle as many as you can.

You may also discover that you have stories about other people
Here are some examples:

- People are so rude
- Everyone's out for themselves
- They're all a bunch of show-offs
- All politicians are liars

Write down your stories about other people.

We'll come back to these stories in a later chapter.

Positive stories are just as limiting
Maybe you don't relate to any of the stories I listed above. Try these instead:

- I'm doing my best
- I'm a winner
- I'm successful
- I make things happen
- I'm really intelligent
- I'm creative
- Everyone looks up to me
- People are counting on me
- I'm the life and soul of the party
- I don't take no for an answer
- I always get what I want
- I'm an entrepreneur
- I'm an achiever
- I'm driven
- I'm a good father / mother

These stories may sound wonderful, but they're based on the same misunderstanding as the first list. The misunderstanding is that individual mental and physical effort makes things happen. Hence the phrase, "If it is to be, it's up to me".

This book is based on the premise that we're part of something bigger and infinitely intelligent. Each of us can tune into it if we want to. That's why letting go works so much better than trying to achieve everything through mental and physical effort. I'll explain this in detail as we go along.

Letting go isn't about sitting in a yoga pose on a beach or in a cave somewhere. It's about abandoning your attempts to control what happens. This allows things to happen in a much more intelligent way. You do less and achieve more.

Some of us have to reach a state of exhaustion, illness and/ or poverty before we let go. Then things *really* start to happen:

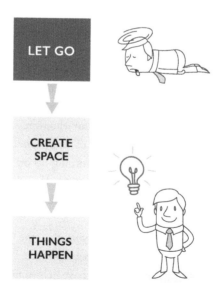

How I began to let go

I was living with my girlfriend in Paris. We were running a business that involved large numbers of self-employed people. For several years my goal had been to earn a certain income, which was almost twice as much as I'd ever earned before. However, I never got anywhere close.

Have you ever had days when nothing goes right? I was having lots of them. I also had that borderline feeling of depression that haunts so many people. Our business in France had ground to a halt. We were earning nothing. There were lots of strikes, including on the Métro. More people than ever were driving to work, so Paris was clogged with traffic jams. Our relationship was falling apart and I had sciatica.

We had barely enough money to pay for groceries. Although I'd been working really hard for years, I felt completely stuck. Deep down, I knew I didn't know what to do. Psychologists call this *conscious incompetence*.

As the Buddhist saying goes, "When the student is ready the teacher appears". The teacher can adopt some unexpected guises. In my search for a new business opportunity, I was working through a course on futures and options trading written by Ken Roberts, an American who wore a cowboy hat in most of his photographs. On one of the tapes he congratulated a small group of participants for turning up on a Sunday morning, to hear him talk about the mind. The others had skipped this session, because it wasn't about the 'hard' skills of analysis and trading.

Ken started off by saying that the mind made all the difference between success and failure. I felt I already knew this, but it didn't seem to have helped much. He then went on to say that successful trading required us to *let go* of the unhelpful thoughts that circulate in the mind. This was something new.

Odd as it may sound, this was a turning point for me. Although I didn't totally understand what he was saying, I did grasp the underlying point. I'd been trying to succeed in life by working on the *outside:* trying to orchestrate people and events to achieve what I wanted. He was talking about turning *inwards*, dealing with the mind first and foremost, and *letting go*.

I gave up learning about futures and options, but I did read some of Ken's other books, including a novel[3] in which he said that, "The mind cannot rise above what it already knows". He also used phrases such as "return to now" and "now knows". I started doing what he described in the novel. Whenever I noticed that my attention had wandered, I brought it gently back to my breath or to one of my senses. Within a couple of weeks I'd developed the habit of bringing my attention back to the present over and over again in the way he described. I was present for longer and longer periods.

I began to feel much better, despite all the difficulties I faced. Then I stood back from the situation and looked at what was happening. For years I'd been attempting to make things happen through thinking and hard work. It had become more and more stressful, producing worse and worse results.

The social scientist in me found this interesting. I was very well qualified and had been working hard for years. Realistically, I couldn't work any harder. However, I was getting nowhere.

This suggested to me that I was doing something fundamentally wrong. If I could find out what it was and change it, my life was likely to improve quickly.

It occurred to me to let go. I stopped making business appointments. I gave up trying to get people to do things. Whenever I noticed that my attention had wandered, I brought it gently back to the present. It was happening over and over again each day, more and more frequently. I noticed that the more I did this, the stronger my intuition became. I just had a feeling about what I should do next. I was also observing my thoughts and feelings, and beginning to understand myself and other people much better.

Having been to church and Sunday school between the ages of five and fifteen, I was in the habit of praying. Many of us pray for certain things to happen in our lives. In this case I simply prayed to be guided to the right job or business. Then I let go.

I also began to explore other career options. A couple of ideas occurred to me, one of which was executive search, otherwise known as 'headhunting'. I'd been very interested in it a few years earlier. At that time I felt I lacked the intuition required to be any good at evaluating people. But now my intuition had become much stronger, I felt ready to take another look.

A short while later, an advertisement appeared in the recruitment section of *The Sunday Times*. Heidrick & Struggles, the world's second-largest search firm, was looking for consultants with the potential to become partners. The salary on offer was more than the annual income I'd been trying and failing to reach for five years. Right now my income was zero.

I replied to the advertisement and, over the next few weeks, had interviews with a total of sixteen partners in London and Paris. Each interview lasted around an hour, with many of the partners asking the same questions. Knowing how to remain present was a big advantage. Before each meeting I placed my attention on my breath and then on each of my senses. This enabled me to listen attentively for an hour at a time.

At one point I had some interviews with another global search firm. It was an obvious place for me to work. They employed lots of MBAs, including several from INSEAD, where I had studied. But they eventually turned me down on the grounds that they didn't need someone like me to win new clients for them. At first I felt frustrated, but then I remembered to let go. I asked to be guided and kept returning to the present, over and over again.

A few weeks later Heidrick & Struggles offered me a job, which I accepted. The base salary was 98% of the amount I'd been trying and failing to earn for several years. There was also a guaranteed first-year bonus which took me significantly beyond that. My goal had become reality, not through dogged hard work but by being present, asking to be guided and letting go. Having been stuck for a long time, I had suddenly made rapid progress.

A few months after joining the firm, I stumbled upon a memo from the chairman, John Viney, to the staff in the London office. He informed them of the decision to recruit some new consultants just below partner level. He also described what the firm was looking for, listing five criteria.

It was uncanny: I matched all of them. It was a perfect fit. In six months I'd gone from a failing business to the perfect job with a company I'd never heard of. After years of struggle I'd suddenly reached my goal by letting go.

I had to hit rock bottom before I stopped trying to control what was happening. Once I let go, my life changed rapidly for the better. What felt like a very painful experience turned out to be a blessing in disguise.

Please note: *you* don't have to wait for things to get this difficult before you let go. You can start letting go now, right where you are.

You could argue that my experience in Paris and London isn't statistically significant: it was one person's experience among many. However, it was highly significant for me. It transformed my life. It also pointed me towards a new way of living, which I have followed ever since. In the meantime I've met many other people who've let go and allowed their lives to change rapidly for the better. My aim in writing this book is to help a very large number of people do the same. I hope you'll be one of them.

3

Stand Back and Observe
Thoughts as They Come and Go

It turned out that I'd learned to meditate by accident. Meditation is the single most useful tool for letting go.

The year after my experience in Paris, Eckhart Tolle's book *The Power of Now*[1] was published. It became an international best seller. Since then, millions of people all over the world have learned a meditation technique known as *mindfulness.*

> **Mindfulness** has been taught by Buddhists for over 2,000 years. According to my friend Shamash Alidina, author of *Mindfulness for Dummies*[2], it has four aspects: presence, compassion, acceptance and curiosity.
>
> Mindfulness requires no religious beliefs, and has been popularised in the West by Jon Kabat-Zinn[3] and others. Approximately 2,500 research papers have been published on the subject.

Eckhart doesn't use the word mindfulness, which he regards as a mistranslation. In any event, we don't need to concern ourselves with curiosity, acceptance or compassion right now. We'll come back to them later. For the time being we'll focus on being present.

Being present means paying attention to the present moment
Being present doesn't mean being physically present, since you're physically present all the time. It's only your attention that wanders. Buddhists call this the *monkey mind.* Left to its own devices, our attention runs around, out of control.

Being present means paying attention to the present moment. Be here now. It sounds simple, but putting it into practice requires a specific technique.

Maybe you've tried to meditate, but it didn't work for you
I meet lots of people who've tried to meditate, but say it didn't work for them. I'll show you how meditation works, and help you find the technique that works for you.

To understand what we're dealing with, try this:

Sit in a quiet place where you won't be disturbed. Switch off your phone. Close your eyes. For the next five minutes, stop thinking.

How did you get on? You'll probably find it impossible to stop thinking for more than a few seconds. Then a thought appears. Then another. Then another. Pretty soon you're thinking about the past, the future, or what may be happening somewhere else right now.

A common misconception is that meditation is about emptying the mind. For most people that's an impossible task – at least initially. So what's the answer?

The secret of meditation is to give the mind something to do
Here's a simple way to get started:

Sit in a quiet place where you won't be disturbed. Switch off your phone. Take off your watch and place it next to you. Close your eyes.

Now turn your attention inwards. Place your attention on your breath as it flows slowly in and out of your body.

Every time your attention wanders, bring it gently back to the breath. There's no need to judge yourself. This is all part of the process. Just bring your attention back to the breath.

Carry on doing this for several minutes.

Now open your eyes. What do you notice? How do you feel? Are the sounds, colours or shapes any different?

Some of us find that colours are brighter. Many of us feel calmer. Sounds or shapes may become clearer. You may notice other sensations throughout your body.

This exercise involves giving your mind something to do, which is to keep paying attention to the breath as it flows in and out. Every time the attention wanders, the mind's job is to bring the attention back to the breath.

There's no need to judge yourself when your attention wanders. It's all part of the process. You just bring your attention gently back to the breath.

You may find yourself thinking about the issue you decided to work on when you read the introduction to this book. Unfortunately, having the same thoughts over and over again won't help much. For now, all you have to do is notice those thoughts, and then bring your attention gently back to your breath. (Later on I'll show you how to deal with the *cause* of those thoughts.)

One of the immediate benefits of doing this exercise is that it gives your mind a rest.

You can now extend the exercise from your breath to your five senses. Try this:

Find a quiet place where you won't be disturbed.

Sit upright on a chair, remaining completely relaxed. Place your hands on your thighs and your feet flat on the floor.

Close your eyes.

Allow your body to relax. Let go of any tension. Let go of any concerns or preoccupations.

Place your attention on the breath as it flows in and out. Every time your attention wanders, bring it gently back to the breath.

Now feel the pressure of the air against your face. Remain aware of this for a while.

Now feel the weight of your body pressing down into the chair. Remain aware of this for a while.

Every time your attention wanders, bring it gently back to the weight of your body pressing down into the chair.

Now feel your feet pressing down into the floor. Remain aware of this for a while.

Listen as far as possible into the distance, beyond the sounds nearby. Remain aware of this for a while.

Let go of any mental comments or judgments about the sounds.

Now bring your attention back to the breath as it flows in and out. Every time your attention wanders, bring it gently back to the breath.

While you were doing the last two exercises, you may have noticed now and then that there weren't any thoughts. You were conscious, but there were no thoughts. It may only have lasted a second or two. As soon as you realise "I've stopped thinking", that's another thought.

It's fine to glance at your watch occasionally while you're meditating. Then you can bring your attention back to the breath. When people meditate in groups, there's often someone who keeps track of time, ringing a bell at the beginning and the end.

Some people get started using only a book. There are also lots of teachers, courses and apps that you may find helpful. I have listed some of them in the Appendix.

Being present will help you observe thoughts and let them go

Many of us behave as though we <u>are</u> our thoughts. We have a happy thought, so we feel happy. We have a sad thought, so we feel sad. Then we act out our thoughts and feelings. It's like being a puppet on a string. Being controlled by our thoughts gets us into all kinds of trouble, ranging from lost career opportunities to broken relationships to road rage.

The solution is to stand back from your thoughts and observe them as they come and go. Being present will help you do this.

Maybe you're feeling stressed about what someone has said, or about a problem you can't solve. Maybe you're on a crowded train, getting frustrated with the physical discomfort or other people's behaviour. In all these situations it's natural to experience a stream of thoughts and feelings.

The question is: what are you going to do about them? Are you going to react by becoming sarcastic, angry or violent? Or are you going to do something different this time? If you let go of those thoughts and feelings, you will create a space for something new to happen.

Try this:

Close your eyes if it's safe to do so. If not, place your attention on an object in front of you. Now feel the breath moving slowly in and out of your body. Feel your weight on the chair, or the pressure of your feet on the floor. Feel the texture of whatever your hands are pressing against.

Every time your attention wanders, bring it gently back to one of your senses. If you have an angry thought, or a feeling of frustration, notice it and then bring your attention back to your senses.

Please note that we aren't denying or repressing thoughts or feelings that arise. We're simply noticing them and bringing our attention back to our senses. Now try this:

Notice each thought as it appears.

Don't try to do anything about it. Don't judge it, resist it or try to push it away.

Just observe it.

In due course the thought will disappear. At some point another thought will come. Just let them come and go.

Being present will help you avoid decisions which you later regret

Remember what Carl Jung said: "Until you make the unconscious conscious, it will direct your life and you will call it fate". The more you practise being present, the easier it'll be to observe thoughts and then decide whether you're going to act on them. You'll become more and more aware of what's going on in your mind. You'll be less and less a victim of 'fate'.

Being present reduces stress

Stress can be defined as *resisting what is*. We judge whatever's happening as wrong. Then we get frustrated, angry or depressed about it. Unfortunately, this reduces our ability to do anything constructive.

If we keep our attention in the present, the stress begins to fade away. Then we can take the appropriate action.

(INSERT OTHER PEOPLE'S EXAMPLES.)

Being present helps us let go of fear

Many people have a fear of heights while climbing a ladder or making their way along a mountain ledge. Some overcome it by placing their attention on the breath and on the sensations beneath their hands and feet. This moves their attention away from fearful thoughts, so they feel calmer and more relaxed. At the same time, they're focused on what really matters – where they're placing their hands and feet.

(INSERT OTHER PEOPLE'S EXPERIENCES.)

Being present makes relationships less stressful

When we allow thoughts to come and go, our relationships change. We no longer react to other people's moods and behaviour in the same old ways.

A few months after I'd learned to be present, I was working on an assignment for the chairman of a company. He was talented and successful, but also moody. Occasionally he would fly into a rage with no warning. The people around him were often stressed. Many of them resigned after a few months of working for him.

One day his secretary phoned me and said he wanted to see me. Apparently he was very angry. If this had happened a year or two earlier, I would have been distracted by thoughts about why he might be angry and what the implications might be. I would have mulled them over on the way to his office, imagining how the conversation would turn out, and what might happen as a result.

Instead, I remembered what I'd learned and placed my attention on the breath, feeling it move slowly in and out of my body. As I walked along the corridor, I felt the temperature and pressure of the air around me and observed the surroundings in detail. When I arrived at his office, my attention was in the present. I was able to listen and reply without any fear or anticipation. The conversation flowed smoothly and easily. We agreed on the action to be taken, without any argument or criticism.

Before learning to be present:

After learning to be present:

Now it's your turn:

Think of a situation where you often get stressed.

Now you have a choice between (a) allowing your mind to run wild and create stories, and (b) remaining present by keeping your attention on your breath, your senses and your surroundings.

Try (b) next time.

I noticed that the less I reacted to other people's moods, the more my relationships improved. I was responsible for my thoughts and feelings. They were responsible for theirs. I no longer rose to the bait.

It may feel strange at first when you stop reacting to other people's moods. It may even feel selfish or inconsiderate. However, we can still love people and have compassion for them. It's their anger and frustration that cause them to suffer, both mentally and physically. Letting go creates space for new relationships with the people around us. They will see the change in our behaviour and may also change theirs.

You don't have to join in the drama
I was once introduced to an American company which needed a new chief executive. I invited a senior partner in the London office to work on the assignment with me.

One afternoon I was in my office when there was a sudden outbreak of violence in the United States. I sent an email to the client commenting on what was happening and updating him on the assignment. I also sent a copy of the email to the senior partner, who then came into my office, furious at what I'd written. He accused me of insensitivity at a time of national trauma in the US.

He sat in front of me, fuming and criticising me bitterly. I was shocked at first, but I sat and listened carefully, feeling my breath as it flowed in and out, and the weight of my body on the chair. Eventually he sighed, shrugged his shoulders and left.

Then I called the client. We talked about what was happening in the US. We talked about the assignment. He was perfectly happy, so we got on with the job.

Being present makes our work much easier
Knowing how to be present and avoid conflict helped me to keep my job at Heidrick & Struggles. After four years I was promoted to partner. I left on good terms a year later.

Since then there have been several occasions that could have been stressful but weren't, such as taking legal action to recover money that was owed to me. Business is much easier once we learn to be present and are no longer at the mercy of our thoughts and emotions.

(INSERT OTHER PEOPLE'S EXAMPLES.)

Stand back. Watch the thoughts and feelings go by
You may find that thoughts and feelings come thick and fast, particularly if someone has criticised you or tried to harm you. If so, it's best to stand back from it all. Try this:

Imagine you're standing on a bridge, gazing down into a river in full flood. The swirling water is your mind in chaos. The water level begins to rise and the river becomes more and more dangerous, carrying all kinds of debris with it. There are branches of trees, wooden planks, car tyres and so on.

The debris is your thoughts and emotions. There can be memories of someone's critical remarks, maybe a few negative thoughts about yourself, thoughts about what might go wrong, and so on. The thoughts are accompanied by emotions such as anger, sadness, regret or a feeling that you're not good enough. They all come sweeping down the river.

There's no need to reach down and hold onto them. If you do so, you may be dragged along and swept away. All you have to do to stay on the bridge is be present. Feel the weight of your body pressing down on the bridge. Feel the breath flowing in and out of your body. Feel the sensations within your body. If you're standing while you do this exercise, stand with your feet slightly apart. Observe the thoughts and emotions as they pass beneath you. Imagine you're resting your hands on the wall of the bridge, looking down into the water. Imagine the sensation of the stone beneath your hands.

Whenever you become distracted, bring your attention back to the breath. Breathe slowly and deeply. Place your attention within your body. Observe the thoughts and emotions. Allow them to come and go.

Letting go of thoughts improves our relationships and helps us to build new ones

When we're listening to what someone is saying, many of us have thoughts about what to say in response, what we would do in their situation, or how we can help them. However well-intentioned these thoughts may be, we aren't really listening. It's better to keep returning to the present when you're with someone. The first step is to make sure you're present before you meet them. You can pause, to make sure you're present, just before a meeting, a party or a meal with a friend. If you're present when you begin, it makes it easier to keep returning to the present while you're with them. Thich Nhat Hanh[4] puts it like this: "The most precious gift we can offer anyone is our attention."

Next time you're listening to someone, feel the breath moving in and out of your body at the same time. It will help to prevent your attention from wandering.

The more we let go of thoughts, the more space we create in our relationships:

(INSERT OTHER PEOPLE'S EXPERIENCES.)

Being present will make you more effective – at work and at play

A few months after I'd learned to be present, my colleagues and I attended an offsite meeting in Cannes on the French Riviera. One day we drove into the hills for an afternoon of sports that included shooting with air rifles. I hadn't used a gun for many years, so this was the first time I'd done so since learning to be present. The difference was remarkable. I felt the breath flowing gently in and out of my body and allowed the thoughts to fall away. Then, after one of the out-breaths, I squeezed the trigger. I did this several times. Suddenly I was a much better shot.

Some sports people experience *the zone,* in which everything seems to slow down. They instinctively make the right move at the right time, without thinking about it. Here's an example from a friend who's a keen golfer:

"I remember that day 10 years ago as if it was yesterday. It was my birthday and a close friend and I had decided to spend the entire day playing golf together. The plan was to play nine holes in the morning, break for lunch, and play another 18 in the afternoon.

The morning game was another ordinary round. However, it allowed me to develop a good feel for the course, and to visualise the fairways and greens clearly. Trusting the feel and knowledge of the course I'd acquired in the morning, we set off to play in the afternoon with a carefree mindset.

I remember being in a very quiet place. There was no internal dialogue, and no criticism or judgment. The focus was on letting go of the score and the scorecard and just experiencing and being in the moment. Everything seemed to happen naturally and instinctively, a little like being in cruise control. It was the lowest score I'd ever shot."

Being present gives you presence

The same principle applies if you're going to speak to a large audience:

Make sure you're present before going on stage or on camera. You will literally have more presence and connect with your audience. Feel the weight of your feet on the floor and place your attention on your breath now and then. This will help to ensure that you aren't carried away by your own material.

The more you remain present, the more other people will pay attention to you and what you're saying.

4

A Whole Load of Things You Can Let Go

Once you've learned to be present - and then stand back and observe your thoughts - you can start letting go of them. You may be wondering why you should do this. The answer is that thoughts clog the system and prevent things from happening. Here's a list to help you get started. These are all repetitive thoughts. We have them over and over again:

- Labels
- Judgments
- Opinions
- Fantasies
- Expectations
- Conclusions
- Conspiracy theories

Repetitive thoughts prevent us from absorbing information and exploring possibilities. They block our intuition and stop useful ideas from coming to us. When we let go of these repetitive thoughts, we create space for things to happen in new and exciting ways.

The stories I've described so far consist of various repetitive thoughts strung together. Letting go of the thoughts helps us to let go of the stories.

Let go of labels

Many of us have a habit of labelling ourselves and other people. We say, "She's a finance person" or "I'm not an entrepreneur". In my work I sometimes meet people who've done a Myers-Briggs[1] test and tell me – without my asking – that they're 'an ENTJ'. The test provides 16 boxes and they've jumped into one of them.

Labelling ourselves and other people is futile. Each of us has enormous potential which we've yet to explore. Labels restrict what we see. Sometimes we only understand this when people apply labels to us. Then we feel how limiting they are.

Think back to the last time someone labelled you. How did you feel about it?

Letting go of labels allows people and situations to change. Then things happen more easily.

Let go of the habit of labelling yourself

In chapter 2 I gave you a list of stories we tell ourselves. Some of them are labels such as *winner*, *loser*, *achiever* and *victim*. There are many other possibilities.

Write down a list of the labels you've applied to yourself.

There could be lots of them. Now put your pen down, stop and look at what you've written. For each label ask yourself the following questions:

- *Can I be 100% certain that this is true?*
- *Is there some pay-off from labelling myself in this way? If so, what is it?*
- *What's the cost of labelling myself? When have I lost out by doing so?*

Now imagine that you've let go of this label. How do you feel?

(INSERT EXAMPLES OF HOW PEOPLE SAY THEY FEEL.)

Let go of the labels that other people have applied to you
This is the second stage. People may say you're clever, stupid, good-looking, ugly, kind, unkind, and so on. If we pay attention to all these labels we can end up very confused. Turn to a fresh page and try this:

Make a list of the labels that other people have applied to you:
Again, there could be lots of them. Now put your pen down, stop and look at what you've written. For each label ask yourself the following questions:

- *Can I be 100% certain that this is true?*
- *Is there some pay-off for other people from labelling me in this way?*

Let go of the habit of labelling others
Now for the third and final stage:

Make a list of people you've labelled in some way, one below the other, down the left-hand side of the page. You can include both individuals and groups of people who share a particular nationality, race or social background.

Now write down the labels you've assigned to each of them. Put your pen down, stop and look at what you've written. Ask yourself the following questions:

- *Can I be 100% certain that these labels are true?*
- *Is there some pay-off from labelling people in this way?*
- *How might these people feel if they find out I've labelled them in this way?*
- *What is the cost of labelling these people? When have I lost out by doing so?*

Letting go of labels creates space for everyone. Relationships improve. Things change.

Avoid labelling those who disagree with you as irrational

When you have a clearly articulated point of view, it's tempting to label anyone who doesn't agree with you as irrational. The implication is that they're driven purely by emotions or prejudice.

This is a common mistake in relationships, business and politics. If you fall into this trap you may find yourself misinterpreting situations, jumping to the wrong conclusions and getting stuck instead of moving forwards.

When they first encountered suicide bombers in the Middle East, some members of the US military labelled them as irrational. The suicide bombers clearly had different values, since they were much more willing to kill civilians. They also had different assumptions from the Americans about the requirements for being admitted to heaven. However, given their values and assumptions, the suicide bombers *were* being rational. They thought they were taking a short cut to paradise.

If we avoid labelling people, and make more effort to understand their values and assumptions, we'll have a much clearer picture of what's really happening. Then we can do something about it.

There are many reasons why people could disagree with you and still be rational. Here are some examples:

- Their values may be different from yours
- You and they may have made different assumptions
- They may have had an experience which you haven't had
- They may have information which you don't have, or have chosen to ignore.

Instead of labelling people, it's better to be curious. I'll talk about that in chapter 10.

Let go of judgments
Many of us label people, events and experiences as 'good' or 'bad'. In other words, we *judge*. However, these mental labels don't exist physically. As Hamlet said in Shakespeare's play of the same name, "…there is nothing either good or bad, but thinking makes it so".[2]

If you judge, you suffer
Most of us have experienced anger or frustration when we felt that 'things shouldn't be this way'.

Here's a simple example. You believe it should be sunny at this time of year, but it rains, so you judge the weather as bad. In reality, it's raining. Judging the weather as bad can only cause you stress. (Living in a country such as Britain provides endless opportunities to learn this lesson.)

In this case the suffering may be minor, but the same principle applies to other judgments. We can spend years judging family members, colleagues, politicians, nationalities, ethnic groups, and so on. *If you judge, you suffer*. While we suffer we're unable to do anything very constructive.

Judgments are a waste of time

Most of us have had an experience which we labelled at the time as 'bad', 'frustrating', 'a waste', 'a mess' or similar, but have then been delighted with the final outcome. Something we found distressing at first turned out to be extremely helpful. In executive search I can think of several candidates who failed to get a particular job, and went on to be enormously successful elsewhere. They're now happy and relieved to have 'failed' along the way.

There's a Chinese proverb known as *The Old Man from the Border Loses a Horse*, which has often been adapted in the West. It illustrates the futility of judging.

During the Han Dynasty, an old man named Sai Weng lived near the border. One day he lost his horse. His neighbours said this was very bad luck and sympathised with him. But he said, "Maybe losing my horse is not so bad after all".

The next day the horse returned, with a beautiful mare (female horse). The neighbours said this was good luck, but Sai Weng said, "Maybe this is not such good luck after all'. His son loved the mare and rode her every day. One day she was startled by a wild animal and threw him from her back. He broke his leg and couldn't walk. The neighbours said, 'What bad luck!' But the old man said, 'Maybe it's not such a bad thing after all'.

Then a war broke out on the frontier. The Emperor's army passed through the border region and recruited all the young men who were able to fight. Because Sai Weng's son had a broken leg, he couldn't join the army and was left in the village to work on the farm with his father.

Sai Weng said to his neighbours, "Being thrown from the horse saved my son from almost certain death in the war, so it all worked out in the end."

In China, when something looks like bad news, someone often says, "Sai Weng Shi Ma" meaning, "The old man from the border loses a horse".[3]

The more we return to the present, the easier it is to observe judgments as they appear. Then we can let go of them and allow something new to happen. Here's an exercise which can help us drop the habit of judging what happens:

As you carry out your activities throughout the day, observe what goes on around you. This includes the way people speak and behave, the weather, the pace at which things happen or don't happen, the thoughts which appear in your mind, and so on.

If you keep returning to the present, as I described in chapter 3, you'll start to notice judgments appearing in your mind. Examples include, "she shouldn't have said that", "people shouldn't do that", "what a stupid situation" and so on.

Instead of clinging to them, see if you can let them come and go. It's important not to resist them, since that makes it harder to let them go.

Fairly soon these judgements will vanish. New thoughts will appear. You can then let go of them too.

Let go of opinions

Here's a revealing exercise which I use in workshops. You can try it for yourself. First of all I pick some controversial questions, such as the following:

Should ordinary citizens be allowed to carry guns?

Should immigration be stopped?

Should everyone be vegetarian?

Should hunting be allowed?

I imagine you can think of other questions that are likely to arouse strong emotions. The second step is to ask the participants to raise their hands (a) if they're strongly in favour and (b) if they're strongly against. Then I pair them up: for and against.

Now for the third step. One person (the talker) spends five minutes explaining, in the strongest possible terms, why they're in favour of a particular idea. The other person (the listener) is asked to:

- Listen attentively, without speaking, for the full five minutes
- Say nothing
- Let go of any opinion that appears in his or her mind
- Keep listening.

After five minutes they switch roles. The second person talks. The other listens. This is how one participant described the experience: (INSERT EXAMPLE.)

Let go of opinions for 48 hours
You can try this exercise on your own:

For the next 48 hours, have no opinions.

During each conversation, listen intently to what the other person is saying. Give them your full attention.

Every time you notice an opinion coming up, let it go. Discard it. Carry on listening.

When s/he has finished speaking, either remain silent or ask a question so you can understand what s/he has said in more detail.

Source: The Kabbalah Centre

How did you get on? What happened in your mind and your body during this exercise? Write it down in your notebook.

This is how one participant described the experience: (INSERT)

This exercise helps us to observe thoughts and feelings as they well up inside us, which brings us to the subject of fantasies.

Let go of fantasies

For several years I rented an apartment in an affluent part of London, and also worked there most of the time. When I first moved there it was common to see Porsches parked in the street. However, the local car population gradually became more and more exotic, including Aston Martins, Ferraris and Lamborghinis.

One day I was walking down the street when I stopped and looked more closely at a Ferrari parked on the side of the road. As I looked at it, I realised that all kinds of thoughts were appearing in my mind. They weren't to do with not having a car. I have little interest in them. They were to do with money, or rather my lack of ready cash at that time. I felt frustrated. I wondered if I would ever have plenty of money again.

But I kept looking at the car, more and more carefully, without moving. After a while I realised that I was looking at some metal, painted red, and some tyres made of black rubber. There was also a little yellow badge with a black horse rearing up on its hind legs. That was all.

Then I repeated the experiment with other objects. I saw a house that was being built. Then I noticed a baby being pushed along in a buggy on the other side of the street. This provoked another flurry of thoughts and emotions. I was living on my own. A lot of my friends were married with children. They owned apartments or houses. I felt as though I had somehow missed a stage in life.

Every time these thoughts and emotions appeared, I carried on looking at the object itself: a house under construction or a baby in a buggy. Eventually I had a feeling of space, with no thoughts or emotions. I could see a house and a baby in a buggy. That was all.

Now it's your turn:

Whenever an object catches your attention, look at it more closely.

Do you see the object for what it is, or are you distracted by thoughts about something else?

Whatever the thoughts may be, keep looking. Eventually they'll die down. You'll begin to see the object for what it is.

In the next chapter I'll show you how to let go of the suffering that causes these fantasies.

Let go of 'shoulds'

Many of us feel we should *be* this or that. Or *do* this or that. Or *have* this or that. When reality doesn't correspond to our *shoulds*, we judge ourselves and feel bad. We often don't realise we're doing it. Try this:

Sit in a quiet place and make a list of all the things you feel you should be, do or have. Here are some ideas to help you get started:

I should have done that.

I shouldn't have done that.

I should have a degree.

I should be married.

I should own my own home.

I should be wealthy by now.

I should be more successful in my career.

I should be fitter.

I should be x kilos lighter.

Getting your 'shoulds' down on paper is a good start. Now examine each one carefully. Where did it come from? Did someone say something that stuck in your mind? Did you pick it up from observing or listening to your friends? Or did it come from someone in authority?

If you examine your shoulds carefully, they will start to lose their power over you.

Now stand up, close your eyes and shake your body, particularly your hands and your feet. Shake off all the shoulds.

Now brings your attention back to the present. Notice how you feel.

It can take a while to let go of your shoulds. Keep shaking them off.

How do you feel?

Let go of expectations – and be surprised

By definition, expectations aren't real. They're repetitive thoughts about how things should be. If things don't turn out the way we expect – or if people don't behave the way we expect – then we feel sad, angry, frustrated, etc.

It isn't always easy to observe our expectations. That doesn't prevent them from causing us pain and getting in the way. Sometimes coaching helps:

One afternoon I was having a conversation with a friend named Darius[4]. I'd told him I was stuck, so we met up to see if we could 'unlock something', as he put it. He listened a lot and then said, "What would you do if you were kind to yourself?" Then he disappeared for a few minutes. It was a sunny afternoon in early September and I gazed up at the buildings nearby. The first thing that came to mind was that I would take more photographs. Then it dawned on me: I would let go of my expectations.

Later that day, I reflected on the times in my life when I had few if any expectations. Exciting things had happened, often quite smoothly. Since then I had accumulated expectations, some of which were unfulfilled. I realised they were making me miserable, so I resolved to let go of them. I immediately felt much better.

Now it's your turn:

Take a blank sheet of paper. Make a list of everything you expect to happen.

Turn over the page. Write down how you expect people to behave, assigning specific expectation(s) to each person.

This exercise may strike you as absurd. It is. Can you see that all these expectations are just thoughts you've had over and over again? They may be *legitimate* expectations, backed up by law or social convention, but they're still just thoughts. They aren't reality.

You can tell people what you want them to do. You can enter into contracts with them. You can take the appropriate action if they don't stick to their commitments. But, if you cling to your expectations about how they'll behave, then <u>you're</u> the one who's going to suffer. Try this instead:

Let go of expectations.

Continue with your work and relationships in the normal way. Tell people what you want them to do. Enter into written agreements with them, if appropriate. Tell them what you're going to do, and then do it. But drop your expectations.

Instead, observe everything that happens, moment by moment, both inside you and all around you.

How do you feel? Do you notice any difference in the way life unfolds?

Letting go of expectations creates space for people and situations to change, and for new things to happen.

Let go of conclusions
Conclusions are closely related to labels and judgments. We have some experiences and conclude – for example – that "Men are like this", "Women are like that", or "That's the way the world is". We conclude that certain things always work in certain ways.

The Latin root of the verb *to conclude* means *to shut completely*[5]. When we reach a conclusion about someone or something, we shut out all other possibilities. This leads to difficulties and lost opportunities. For example, if you conclude that everyone from a particular national, religious or ethnic group behaves in a certain way, you may treat a person from that group unfairly. You may also lose a potential friendship or business opportunity.

Many of us have developed a list of conclusions that are now shaping our lives. In some cases, we're no longer aware of what's going on. Remember what Carl Jung said: "Until you make the unconscious conscious, it will direct your life and you will call it fate."

Regular meditation will make you much more aware of what's going on around you. You'll be less likely to jump to conclusions.

The first step in letting go of conclusions is to become conscious of them:

Turn your exercise book or pad of paper sideways (landscape way) so you can write horizontally on four pages. In the top left-hand corner of each page, write one of the following:

1. *The places you don't like*
2. *The kind of people you don't like*
3. *The activities you avoid*
4. *The situations you avoid getting into.*

Now, on the left-hand side of each page, write down the event or events that have led you to this conclusion – one below another.

Now ask yourself the following questions: what is this conclusion costing me? What am I missing in life as a result of this? Write down the answers.

Now look at your list of conclusions again. How would you feel if you let go of them?

The importance of not knowing

Our culture places a big emphasis on knowing. We accumulate knowledge from an early age, and are tested on it. People with a vast amount of general knowledge are celebrated in the media. Not knowing is sometimes seen as failure. Some people pretend to know things when they don't.

However, all knowledge is based on the past. Even language is based on the past, since words have conventional meanings agreed long ago. We can all too easily cling to what we know and fail to see what's happening here and now.

Sometimes we even try to know the unknown, such as when we make economic or financial forecasts. I once met an analyst who worked for a leading investment bank and specialised in the airline industry. She was required to project airlines' earnings years into the future, based on various assumptions about the US dollar and the oil price. Shortly after she wrote one of her reports, the oil price halved. Everything changed.

We may even feel a need to have an answer to personal questions such as "Why did that relationship end?" But in a few months or years we'll see what happened from a different point of view. That doesn't usually stop us from inventing explanations, but they change over time. It also depends on who we're talking to.

If we stop clinging to knowledge – and the need to know – we create space for things to happen in unexpected ways. Life becomes fresh and exciting again.

It's better to admit that you don't know

As it says in the *Tao Te Ching*, "To know that you do not know is the best. To pretend to know, when you do not know, is a disease." [6]

At first, admitting that you don't know may feel like an admission of weakness, even failure. In reality, not knowing can lead to major breakthroughs. Not knowing creates space for us to explore freely. It helps us to let go of old ideas and concepts. We become open to new possibilities.

Sometimes it's better to ask a question and leave it open, instead of rushing to some conclusion. Sir John Templeton, one of the world's most successful investors, created a list of 10 maxims. This is number 10: "No one knows everything. An investor who has all the answers doesn't even understand the questions." [7]

Let go of the need to explain everything

When we experience something we can't explain, it's tempting to start inventing explanations. This happens regularly with some of my friends. No sooner have I finished describing an experience than they leap in with 'rational' explanations. They haven't had the experience themselves, but they have an instant explanation for my experience. Some of us don't need our friends to provide the explanations. We do it for ourselves.

Nassim Nicholas Taleb, the author of *Black Swan*, puts it like this, "Our minds are wonderful explanation machines, capable of making sense out of almost everything and generally incapable of accepting the idea of unpredictability." [8]

It's better to *experience* things with an open mind before trying to understand them intellectually.

Let go of conspiracy theories

Some people *love* conspiracy theories. The mind assembles a story about what has happened or what might happen. It's exciting to gather new information that appears to fit the story.

If you do this you're likely to shut out any information that contradicts your story. You will no longer see things as they are.

You may make decisions which you later regret.

It's better to notice conspiracy theories and let them go, just like any other repetitive thought. (INSERT EXAMPLES)

Don't cling to goals – let them come and go

Goal setting is very popular. Maybe you have some goals of your own. If so, let's consider them one at a time.

Turn to a blank page and write down your goals.

For each goal, please answer the following questions:

- *Where did this goal come from?*
- *Did you pick it up from someone else?*
- *Was it a thought that simply occurred to you?*

Some of us take goals very seriously, but they're just thoughts that appear over and over again. Sometimes we write them down and label them as 'mine'.

But what if something even more amazing happened? Why not be open to every possibility? The more we let go, and the more space we create, the more we realise how limiting goals can be.

Goals usually reflect some underlying desire. There's nothing particularly wrong with desires or goals, but we create problems for ourselves when we *cling* to them. We worry about whether they're going to happen. We start trying to manipulate people and circumstances in order to *make* them happen. It's better to let go and create space for new things to happen.

Here's an alternative approach:

When a thought arises about something you would like to happen – or would love to happen – just notice it. Don't resist it or suppress it. Just allow it to be.

After a while it will disappear and another thought will come.

Notice thoughts as they arise. Notice what's happening around you.

When we let go, we create space for things to happen naturally.

By all means make plans, but don't take them too seriously
Plans are useful in business. They enable us to figure out the resources that will be needed. They help us to understand whether a particular project or company is likely to make money. Then we can decide whether or not to go ahead. Likewise, you may make a plan to go on holiday or find a place to live.

But many people try to plan their entire lives. As Woody Allen put it, "If you want to make God laugh, tell him about your plans." [9]

- **Let Go**
- **Create Space**
- **Things Happen**

5
Let Go of Suffering

In the last chapter I talked about repetitive thoughts such as judgments, labels, fantasies, conspiracy theories and so on. Sometimes all we need to do is notice and observe them. They disappear in due course. But some of them are rooted in painful emotions that provoke negative thoughts over and over again. If we take the time to uncover and *feel* those emotions deeply, they start to lose their power over us. Then the thoughts begin to die down of their own accord.

Feel pain and let it go
Every now and then we feel bad about something that's happening, or anxious about something that may or may not happen. Here are some examples:

- Someone close to you is seriously ill and may die.
- You have no job, no money, or both.
- You're afraid of something that might happen.
- Something you've wanted to happen for a long time still hasn't happened.

Most of us try to avoid negative emotions by doing one of the following. Some of us do both:

a) **We suppress the feeling and try to focus on something positive.** This usually doesn't work. We still feel bad at frequent intervals.

b) **We try to escape the feeling by taking lots of action.**
   This may appear to work for a while, particularly if the action is directed at what we perceive as the external source of the problem. "At least I'm *doing something* about it!" we tell ourselves. However, we still feel bad inside, and other people pick up on our emotions, so our actions don't usually achieve very much.

Negative emotions are the underlying problem

The underlying problem is that negative emotions generate lots and lots of negative thoughts. Sometimes they come so thick and fast that it's very difficult to let go of them in the ways I've described earlier. So what's the solution?

Try this:

The Sofa Exercise[1]

Notice when you feel bad about what's happening, or might happen, or still hasn't happened.

At the earliest opportunity, stop whatever you're doing. Don't take any more action. It probably won't achieve much anyway if you feel bad while you're doing it.

Make yourself a nice warm drink. Sit on a comfortable chair or sofa in a place where you won't be disturbed.

Now close your eyes and find the negative feeling, which will probably be located somewhere in your body.

Now sit and feel it. Keep feeling it.

You may notice judgments about how you feel. Notice how you feel about those judgments. Feel those feelings too.

You may notice labels about your experience. How do you feel about those labels? Feel those feelings too.

Eventually the feelings may begin to die down

This exercise could take a minute or two, or longer in some cases.

If you run out of time, you can come back to it later and continue.

If the negative feeling reappears, you can repeat this exercise. Do so as often as you wish.

After doing this, many people notice they feel lighter. There are usually fewer thoughts, particularly negative ones. Feeling one negative emotion thoroughly, from beginning to end, can remove the cause of hundreds or even thousands of negative thoughts.

When I do this exercise, I usually feel much better afterwards. The circumstances may not have changed, but the torrent of thoughts has been replaced by a feeling of space. Sometimes I then have ideas about a course of action I should take. If I decide to go ahead, I can do so in the knowledge that I'm feeling good, which is one of the ingredients for success.

(INSERT SOMEONE ELSE'S EXPERIENCE.)

Sometimes negative emotions come up during meditation
If they do, it's best to pause and feel them. Eventually they die down. Then we can go back to the meditation.

- Let Go
- Create Space
- Things Happen

6

Discover What Else You Need to Let Go

One of the sneaky things about the junk we carry around in our minds is that we don't always know it's there. In this chapter I'm going to help you find more of it, so you can let it go. I'm going to start by asking you to think about other people. This may seem puzzling at first, but bear with me. All will be revealed.

Who do you find most annoying?

Take a blank sheet of paper. On the left-hand side, make a list of the people you find most annoying, one below another. You can include individuals and types of people. Write down as many as possible.

Now for the second step. To the right of each name on the list, write down what you find most annoying about them.

Please write down as many names as possible. The more data you have to work with, the better.

You will end up with something like this:

Who I find most annoying	What I find most annoying about them
Jack	....
Jill	....
Deepika	....
Hieronymous	....
Etc.	....

Now let me ask you another question:

Do you keep having similar problems with different people?

Write them down:

The problems I keep having with other people are:

....

....

....

....

....

....

Many of the problems we have with other people follow a pattern. One is finding yourself in stressful situations with colleagues, at different times and in different organisations. Another is having a similar, unsatisfactory relationship, with one partner after another. Eventually, some of us realise that the common denominator is us. We can change job, find a new partner or emigrate, but the same things keep happening. Hence the title of Jon Kabat-Zinn's book, *Wherever You Go, There You Are.*

For years I had problems with judgmental people, who kept appearing in my life. At work I seemed to be surrounded by judgmental colleagues. I also had two relationships with women who were highly judgmental. It was entertaining for a while, but ultimately exhausting. Instead of remaining in the present and enjoying life, I had to keep justifying myself.

The people you find annoying have a message for you

You may be shocked to hear me say this, but the things you find annoying in other people are a reflection of <u>you</u>.

> **The Shadow**
> This is a term coined by Carl Jung. Another word for the shadow is the *dark side*. It contains anything you've failed to accept about yourself. You then project it - unconsciously - onto other people. As a result, you keep having the same problems, over and over again. It's up to each of us to understand our shadow, integrate it and become whole. (I'll show you how to do this.) As Jung put it, "I'd rather be whole than good" [1].

The way to understand your shadow is to look at the people who annoy you most – hence the exercise above. What annoys you about them is something you've *suppressed* in yourself and *projected* onto them. You'll keep seeing it in other people until you acknowledge that same aspect of yourself and embrace it.

In my case, those judgmental colleagues and girlfriends were obvious examples. How had I projected being judgmental onto them? Then it dawned on me. *I* was judgmental, sometimes extremely so. I'd denied that I was judgmental and had thereby projected it onto other people. Judgmental people kept appearing in my life as a reminder. They would carry on doing so until I became whole.

Relations with my previous girlfriend had been difficult since we split up. The next time I saw her, I told her I realised I'd been very judgmental, just as she'd always insisted. "Finally" she said. After that our relationship magically improved. Suddenly she was far less judgmental. From then on, fewer judgmental people showed up in my life.

Overweight people also wound me up – particularly men in their forties and fifties. I kept bumping into them, sometimes literally. What was the lesson? Strangely, overweight women didn't bother me.

Then I realised. I'd been trying to lose three or four kilos for ages. I knew I had more energy when I was lighter, and ran better. However, I'd been fighting the fact that I was overweight, instead of embracing it. Hey presto! I was surrounded by overweight men, silently reminding me that I hadn't accepted being overweight.

I experimented with thinking about the subject differently. "I'm overweight" didn't feel too good. I also tried, "I'm heavier than I want to be". That didn't feel great either. It implied I didn't accept myself as I was – I knew that wasn't going to help.

Then I tried, "I <u>can</u> be overweight". That felt much better. It was something I was capable of being. I might or might not be overweight at any particular time. As I experimented with these ideas, overweight men somehow appeared in my life less frequently. Maybe they were there but I wasn't noticing them so much. Within a few weeks people were commenting that my weight had fallen, although I'd made no extra effort. My problems with judgmental men and excess weight receded once I became whole.

As Carl Jung put it, "Everything that irritates us about others can lead us to an understanding of ourselves." [2]

What if the people you find annoying do something you never do?

I've often presented the last two exercises at workshops. On one occasion, a smiling, well-dressed lady in the audience told us about a 'vagabond' who'd muttered something to her as she passed him in the street earlier that evening. When she stopped to hear what he was saying, he blew smoke in her face. She had found this very annoying.

When I asked if she smoked, she said no. Then I asked what she found annoying about this incident. She said she found it annoying because smoking is harmful. It can cause cancer. Then I asked her if she could think of occasions when she'd harmed people. She thought about it for a while and said "I've harmed people sometimes with the words I've used. I've hurt others knowingly or unknowingly."

It takes courage to look inside and face aspects of ourselves that we've suppressed, denied or simply failed to notice. Once we do so, we can embrace them and become whole.

You may have stories about other people

In chapter 2 I talked about letting go of stories about yourself. I also said you might have stories about *other people*. Here are the examples I gave:

- People are so rude
- Everyone's out for themselves
- They're all a bunch of show-offs
- All politicians are liars

Once you identify a story you tell about others, you can turn it into a question about you. For example:

- When have I been rude?
- When have I been selfish?
- When have I been a show-off?
- When have I lied?

Having identified the behaviour you've denied in yourself, you can now embrace it. For example:

- I can be rude
- I can be selfish
- Sometimes I show off
- Sometimes I tell lies

Then you'll become whole. The following story illustrates how this works:

It's time to reclaim your castle

Here's a powerful metaphor to explain the shadow[3]. It encourages us to identify the parts of ourselves that we've suppressed and projected onto other people.

Imagine you're a magnificent castle with hundreds of rooms. Every one of them is perfect and contains a special gift. One room is love, another is creativity. Others include greed, lust, arrogance, honesty and so on. As a child you explore the castle from top to bottom, accepting and enjoying every room.

While you're growing up, visitors tell you that certain rooms in your castle are unacceptable, so you close them off. These visitors include your parents, teachers, religious leaders and so on. Shutting and locking the doors to these rooms makes you feel safe. Before long you're living in just a few small rooms.

Many of us lock the doors to so many rooms that we forget we're a magnificent castle. We begin to believe that we're a small, two-roomed apartment in need of repairs.

However, each room is an essential part of the castle and has its opposite somewhere in the building. We're dissatisfied with being less than we're capable of being, so we begin our search for the other rooms in our castle. We can only become whole by unlocking each door one by one.

As we begin to accept every aspect of ourselves, it becomes easier to accept other people. We realise that many of the things we find annoying about them are projections of something we've suppressed or denied in ourselves. It's also easier to have compassion for them – particularly if they're dealing with something that we've struggled with for years, such as being judgmental or overweight.

The things we judge in other people reflect aspects of ourselves that we've suppressed. Once we acknowledge and embrace them, they lose their power over us. Then we become whole.

Becoming whole creates space for things to happen

When we're trying to be one thing but not another, we experience inner turbulence. It's better to accept that we can be anything and everything. Then we become whole. We can relax. Giving up the fight allows us to let go of so many thoughts that were troubling us. It creates lots of space.

- **Let Go**
- **Create Space**
- **Things Happen**

7
Let Go of the Past

Our thoughts and feelings about the past get in the way of what's happening now. Removing them creates space, so new things can happen.

When small children see something for the first time, they often look at it in amazement, or get closer, so they can examine it more carefully. This includes dogs, cats, flowers, trees, puddles, thunderstorms and sunsets. But by the time we reach adulthood, most of us have collected a list of experiences relating to everything around us, from dogs to sunsets.

When we see a sunset now, or a dog comes up to us, many of us automatically have thoughts about the past. We *associate* what's happening now with some previous experience. If we allow this to continue, we'll only be vaguely aware of what's happening. We're no longer present. For example, when you see a sunset you may start thinking about a holiday a few years ago and who you were with at the time. If a dog comes up to you, you may think about your own dog who died when you were twelve years old, and how sad you were about it.

We may enjoy a particular memory or shudder at the thought of it. But dwelling on it prevents us from being present and experiencing life as it unfolds. Instead, we link or compare what's happening now to some previous event. *Associations* make our lives seem dull and heavy. It's usually easier to observe this in other people than in ourselves. You've probably met someone who reacts to events in the present by talking about something similar in the past.

This habit is particularly unhelpful when we meet new people. It's difficult to get to know them with an open mind if we keep making comparisons with someone from the past. If we start to make these comparisons out loud, it can be very off-putting.

Of course experience is valuable. It helps us to make better decisions. From childhood onwards we learn that dogs may bite, nettles sting and so on. When we do something regularly, we recognise useful patterns. For example, having played tennis for a while, we anticipate how the ball will bounce, and what the effect of a certain stroke will be. Experience provides us with generalisations about what's *likely* to happen in a particular situation.

But fulfilling our potential involves doing new things. The past may give us little or no insight into what we should do now. We can always draw on our experience if it's relevant, but we don't have to keep thinking and talking about it.

For many of us, letting go of the past is easier said than done. Our memories are triggered by people, places and the situations in which we find ourselves. Try this:

Next time you're listening to someone, you may notice that your mind has drawn a comparison with a similar event in the past. Now you have a choice:

- *You could choose to talk about the past. Maybe you can predict the direction the conversation will take if you do that.*

- *You could say nothing about the past. If fact, you could say nothing at all, and then see what happens next. Give it a try.*

What happens now?

This exercise takes practice. At times you may notice yourself responding to what someone has said by talking at length about a similar experience that you've had. Whenever you notice you've done this, you may feel ashamed or embarrassed, but you can simply ask them a question and get them talking again. Then listen and see what happens.

If there's a pause in the conversation, <u>let it be</u>. Something will happen in the space. It needn't be you talking about the past again.

Space is where new things happen

When we stop drawing comparisons with the past we create a space in which something new can happen. This may feel scary at first. Some of us identify strongly with the past: where we were born, our family background, education, work, achievements, etc.

I'm not asking you to forget everything you've learned, or deny the experiences you've had. I *am* saying that it's best to let go of them and experience what's happening *now* with an open mind.

Let go of pain from the past

Most of us have thoughts most of the time. They seem to pop up out of nowhere. Some thoughts lead to negative emotions. Then we have a choice. One option is to push the unpleasant thoughts back down, but they may pop up again at just the wrong time. It's like pushing a football deep underwater. The moment we stop holding it in place it rushes to the surface and leaps out of the water.

Some of us are in the habit of focusing on what we like most about our lives. We're glass-half-full people who don't dwell on the negatives.

You can be as positive as you like. Those painful experiences you've suppressed will still come back up. It may be a sense that things aren't quite right. Or it may be something much more dramatic that causes you to erupt in anger or sink into depression.

The solution is to embrace negative feelings and become whole
I mentioned becoming whole in the last chapter. If you do the work, you can heal pain that goes back years – even decades in some cases. Then things start to happen more smoothly and easily.

You may have experienced becoming whole
If you've ever made a full recovery from bereavement or the end of a relationship, you'll have experienced becoming whole. Here's a personal example.

Ever since my Dad died I've kept a photo of him – taken a couple of months before – in my living room. In the photo it's a sunny day in the orchard at the bottom of my parents' garden. He's sitting in his wheelchair while I'm picking apples and passing them down to him. Despite the Multiple Sclerosis, he's fooling around. In one hand he's holding a homemade apple-picking device consisting of a long stick with the top half of a plastic bottle lashed onto one end. He's talking into it while holding an apple to his ear, pretending it's an old-fashioned telephone.

In the first few weeks after he died, I would cry most times when I saw the photo. In Neuro-Linguistic Programming (NLP), this is known as an *anchor*[1]. An external stimulus – in this case a photograph – triggers an internal response. I knew that anchors could become weaker and sometimes disappear altogether, so I kept the photo in my living room and looked at it several times a day. I allowed myself to feel the grief. Gradually it became easier. There was less pain when I looked at the photo.

That was several years ago. These days I look at the photo and usually feel happy. I appreciate my Dad and the time we spent together.

Can you think of a similar situation in which you embraced your emotions and were gradually healed? There's no right or wrong about this, but it's nice to know your starting-point.

Becoming whole has measurable benefits

When we deal with painful memories we can heal ourselves and lead happier lives. Here's an example described by my friend Dr Norman Rosenthal in his book, *The Gift of Adversity*:

"In 1966, James W. Pennebaker, professor and chair of psychology at the University of Texas in Austin, developed a technique called "the writing exercise", in which people are asked to write down their deepest thoughts and feelings about something that concerns them. In research on this technique, there are typically four sessions of writing, each about twenty minutes long, spread out over several days. The subjects are instructed not to bother about grammar or sentence structure – simply to write. The goal is not the written product or the process of writing itself…."

"By now there have been hundreds of controlled studies on the writing exercise, yielding many intriguing results. A group of Texas Instruments workers, for example, had undergone a harsh layoff: Their unexpected job loss was compounded by an impersonal and insulting process, the kind with security guards escorting them out like thieves. As you can imagine, the workers were angry.

The company then hired an outplacement firm to help them get new jobs. A controlled study of the writing exercise was conducted on a subset of the workers. Those in the control condition were simply asked to write a report of their day's activities, whereas the experimental group was to write about their deepest thoughts and feelings. The outcome: Those in the experimental group found new jobs more quickly than the controls, even though they had made roughly the same number of phone calls and gone to the same number of job interviews." [2]

If you've lost your job or had to close down a business, I encourage you to do this exercise for yourself. It will help you to let go and allow something new to happen.

Becoming whole creates space and allows things to happen

I've attended several programmes run by Paramahamsa Nithyananda[3], on his ashram and elsewhere in India. (*Nithyananda* is a Sanskrit word which means *eternal bliss.* His followers call him *Swamiji.*) The term he uses for becoming whole is *completion*:

"When we carry uncompleted problems we cannot begin anything new. The beliefs and emotions connected with our unfinished troubles continue to create the same difficulties in our future. Once we attain completion our previous patterns are burned and we are set free to initiate a new way of being. Intention is the key to successful completion. When we devote intense, focused time and energy to completing our patterns we evolve and become integrated." [4]

Please note: a *pain pattern* or *incompletion* is a mental impression or psychological imprint that makes us feel powerless. They shape our lives, even though we aren't fully conscious of them.

Here's Swamiji's completion technique[5]:

All you need is a pen, some sheets of paper and a mirror in which you can see your whole face. Sit quietly on your own in a place where you won't be disturbed.

1. *Make a list of incidents or situations in the past that cause you to experience negative emotions in the present. The events could have occurred in any area of your life, at any time between early childhood and the recent past.*

2. *Next to each event, write down the negative emotions you experience now. For example, they could include sadness, grief, anger, guilt, frustration or agitation.*

3. *Sit in a comfortable position facing the mirror. Connect with the person in the mirror. Look directly into their eyes.*

4. *Contemplate the incidents/situations in your life that cause you to experience negative emotions in the present.*

5. *Now take responsibility for liberating yourself from each incompletion that you have kept alive for yourself*

6. *Re-live those incidents/situations. Talk aloud with the person in the mirror. Relive each incident at least five times during an individual session.*

7. *Keep on re-living the incidents/situations. Continue talking again and again until you've let go of the negative emotions inside you.*

Please note that you don't <u>recall</u> the incident. You <u>relive</u> it. If it happened when you were five years old, you become a five-year-old again, with the way you saw things at that age – <u>not</u> the way you see things now. Feel it like a five year old. Then talk to the person in the mirror.

When I first tried this I felt a bit odd talking to myself in a mirror. However, I soon realised it was working. That inspired me to continue. Once I had relived each negative experience five or six times, I would get bored with the story and begin to let go of it. Then it would start to lose its power over me. Some very painful memories required several sessions, on separate days. Gradually, they bothered me less and less.

It can take a lot of work to remove all the pain patterns we've accumulated, but it's well worth it. You don't have to tackle them all at once. You can keep a journal and work on them steadily every day.

In the meantime, it's a good idea to deal with new incompletions as they arise. A practical method is to keep a notebook and write down each painful experience as it occurs. (Please do this on paper rather than on an electronic device. It's much more effective.) Then you can relive them and let go of them each night before you go to sleep. Many people say they sleep much better as a result.

After a few days of reliving each negative experience last thing at night, I gave it a break for a couple of days. I soon noticed that my mind felt a bit clogged by experiences that I hadn't processed. It was as though I'd neglected my mental hygiene. It was like not taking a shower for a couple of days.

I encourage you to persist with the completion technique and practise it every day. You can also attend a seminar and learn in a group, at little or no cost. Please see Further Information at the back of this book.

You may spot your pain patterns while listening to other people

In chapter 4 I described a couple of listening exercises. You may have noticed that listening to someone can trigger thoughts about *you*. These thoughts come from our incompletions – the areas in which we aren't whole. For example, if you're concerned about money, listening to someone talk about their finances may trigger thoughts about *your* financial situation. If you're concerned about your health, then listening to someone talk about their health will probably trigger thoughts about *your* health.

You can use completion to let go of fear

Most of us have fears about what might happen. Different people are afraid of different things. Some are afraid of spiders, while others are afraid of ill health or losing their jobs.

Clearly some fears are rational and help us survive. One example is the fear of wild animals. However, in most cases, if we analyse our fears we find they come from past, negative experiences that may never be repeated. If we can identify those negative experiences, we can remove the pain patterns arising from them. Then we can stop worrying about the future and live our lives to the full. You can start doing this now:

Take a pen and a piece of paper. Sit quietly in a place where you won't be disturbed.

Now identify something you're afraid of. It's probably something that keeps appearing in your mind, even when you're doing something else. Write it down on paper. This will help you to analyse it and deal with it.

Now look carefully and figure out what kind of fear it is. Is it a fear of a particular kind of person, or situation, or difficulty? Whatever it is, it's likely to make you feel powerless, just like any other incompletion.

Now look back over your life and identify when you first felt powerless in this way. Do the completion exercise above. Let the painful memory go when it's ready.

How did you get on? In case you're scratching your head, here's a personal example to help you get started:

I realised I was afraid that a woman I knew would try to get me involved in all kinds of voluntary work, when I was already busy with other things. I wrote a description of this fear on paper and then began to look back over my life to identify other times when I'd experienced a similar fear.

There had been several episodes with women who I felt were bossing me around. I seemed to attract them into my life, but that said more about me than it did about them. However, there was nothing particularly compelling. Then I suddenly remembered rehearsing for a school play when I was about 14 years old. The English teacher kept telling us to turn up at lunchtime and after school for rehearsals. I was busy with my schoolwork and other activities, so I soon got fed up with it. I told her I didn't want to be in the school play any more, at which point she got angry and told me how disappointed she was with me.

That episode occurred decades ago and I'd practically forgotten it. But when I examined it closely, I realised that this particular pattern was still shaping my life and causing me pain.

The good news is that we can deal with these fears and move on. In this case I did the completion exercise as usual. A few days later I spoke to the woman who'd been the subject of my fearful thoughts. We had a friendly conversation and there was no problem at all. I felt liberated.

This is how a friend of mine named Nell described an early experience of completion:

I was flying back to London after visiting my mother in the US when it dawned on me that the 6mg of melatonin I had taken wasn't working. I was wide-awake, listening to the engine on a seven-hour flight. There was also turbulence, which made my stomach sink.

Having been introduced to the completion exercise, I decided to give it a try. It was time I confronted my phobias. Phobias come in different forms. My phobia was of heights – also known as acrophobia - and flying for more than three hours. I've had this fear as long as I can remember. Going to an amusement park is not an option for me.

When I started to do the exercise, locating the source of pain wasn't difficult. It was a churning pain in my stomach. As I tried to re-live it, a painful episode when I was young emerged. There was a building my mum said was downright risky and a friend of mine she always disapproved of, for being too spoilt and unruly. My friend used to come up with daring ideas during playtime. We used to climb onto the roof, six storeys up. The roof was shaped like a ski slope, with a flat piece at the bottom, followed by a six-storey drop. We used to climb up the slope and slide down again to the flat part. If either of us had overshot we would have died.

We probably climbed up there a couple of times, and I knew it was far too dangerous to play there. But I never mentioned it to my parents. I felt guilty. At the same time I didn't want to lose my friend. It was a relief when her family were relocated and I never saw her again. Both our lives could have ended in tragedy.

During this exercise I realised that my phobias stemmed from that time. The two phobias were very much connected and it felt like a heavy stone was being lifted off me. When I tried reliving the episode for the first time, it was so painful my body trembled. Then it got easier on the third try. On my fifth try, I felt something heavy lifting off me. I felt like a bird flying, as though I had grown my broken wing. After that I recalled the incident again and felt no pain at all."

A few weeks later Nell flew from Norway to the United States, via London. The flight was free from pain and fear. The same thing happened on the way back. In fact, she slept well on the overnight flight to London, for the first time in years.

How about you? Which fears do you experience now that are based on events in the distant past?

Your mind may resist liberation

Sometimes, when we're doing the completion exercise, we feel tired or bored, or we get distracted. It's easy to lose count of how many times we've relived a particular episode. We can overcome this by keeping count on the fingers of one hand.

A friend of mine told me the first time she did the completion exercise she had a throbbing headache. However, she knew that painful memories were coming to the surface. She kept going, so she could get rid of them.

Each of us has a root pattern

A *root pattern* arises from a painful experience in early childhood that shapes our lives. Mine suddenly became clear to me during a free webinar that Swamiji gave from India while I was sitting at home in London. This is what happened:

I grew up in England. When I was four we moved less than two hours northwards, from Hertford to Leicester – now famous for the discovery of King Richard III's skeleton beneath a car park.

Although we hadn't moved very far, the local accent was different. It really struck me on my first day at school, at the age of five. Naturally enough, I spoke with the same accent as my parents. At that time, most of the presenters on BBC television had the same accent, so I was used to it. However, it was not the way my young classmates spoke, so they made fun of me. Absurd as it may sound, I chose my accent at the age of five. Faced with rejection at school, I decided to carry on speaking like my parents and the people on the BBC. I was now an outsider.

This outsider mindset stayed with me for decades. Whenever I joined a new group of people, I found myself on the fringe of it. Most of my friends also seemed to be outsiders, in one way or another.

There's a gap between your inner image and your outer image
During my first visit to Swamiji's ashram we did an exercise in which each of us identified our inner image (or self-image) and our outer image, which we project to others.

The experience of being rejected by my five-year-old classmates seemed to have left me with an image of myself as *unacceptable*. My outer image was much easier to identify: "I am clever and friendly". For a couple of hours, 54 of us walked around a room introducing ourselves to each other. In my case I said: "My name is John. I'm unacceptable, but for you I'm clever and friendly". Announcing this to one person after another highlighted the mismatch between the way I saw myself and the way I wanted other people to see me. It had been shaping my life for decades.

Most of us have a mismatch of some sort. If we can close the gap between the way we see ourselves and the way we want others to see us, we can be authentic. The completion exercise can help us do this.

Until we do so, our inner image makes life much more difficult than it needs to be. As you may recall from chapter 6, when we have a strong feeling about ourselves - without being conscious of it - we tend to project it onto other people.

So I projected "I'm not acceptable" onto other people. The result was that other people weren't acceptable to me. Eventually I realised that when I met people for the first time my mind would immediately find a way to dismiss them. It could be their appearance, their accent (that again), their grammar, their attitude, their behaviour. The list went on and on.

Of course, experience had shown over and over again that my prejudices were misguided. In some cases I had become close friends with people whom my mind had initially dismissed. I realised that my relationships and my career were likely to improve significantly if I could drop this whole pain pattern of thinking, feeling and behaving. If I stopped regarding those around me as unacceptable, the world around me was likely to change quickly.

Shortly after I left the ashram I was sitting on a train in southern India, travelling from Chennai to Bangalore. On the opposite side of the aisle from me sat a well-dressed, elderly couple. Every now and then the husband would let out a loud belch, without covering his mouth. I thought to myself, "In the UK that would be totally unacceptable". There was that pain pattern again. I felt I really needed to deal with it. A short while later a baby started crying. The young man sitting next to me seemed to find it annoying, whereas I found it mildly entertaining. Everyone has their own pain patterns.

Completion will help you remain in the present
I encourage you to do the exercises in this chapter for yourself. Help is available at little or no cost.

The completion exercise has much in common with meditation. In meditation, every time we get distracted, we bring our attention back to the breath, the mantra, or whatever we've been taught to do. Likewise, when practising completion using a mirror, our attention naturally starts to wander. You may feel bored and start thinking about something else. The mind will invent any number of ways to prevent you from letting go of your pain patterns. All you have to do is bring your attention back to your eyes in the mirror, and relive the painful experience over and over again. Completion is a powerful tool for letting go.

Completion helps us to create space

After I returned to London I carried on practising completion each day. After a couple of weeks I suddenly noticed that I was no longer regretting the past or worrying about the future. One day, while I was walking across the park to the office, there were almost no thoughts. There was just sunshine, trees and grass – seemingly in brighter colours than before.

I was present. I was still thinking when I needed to. The rest of the time I had an open, expansive feeling: a big, empty space. This was probably my first real glimpse of what Swamiji calls *living enlightenment.* [6]

It lasted for about 24 hours. Then I had a conversation with someone about politics and the state of the economy. Some of the old, negative thoughts began to creep back in. Fortunately, I only had to do the completion exercise a few times to get rid of them and return to that feeling of space.

- Let Go
- Create Space
- Things Happen

8
Let Go of the Urge to Control

Trying to control what happens is stressful. Letting go creates space for things to work out in unexpected ways. Life becomes much more interesting and enjoyable.

Life keeps pushing us to let go
Many of us have been brought up to believe that if we're intelligent and work hard, life will be great. But it turns out that intelligence and hard work aren't enough. Most of us face challenges which – sooner or later – force us to let go.

Sometimes not getting what we want gives us the push we need
As I said earlier, your goals may change. Sometimes everything has to fall apart before we let go and life changes for the better. When I was living in Paris I had lots of goals for a business that was doomed. I didn't get what I wanted. After I let go and created space, things happened quickly.

When I meet someone who's stuck, I feel their pain and frustration, but I know there's something they need to let go. Holding on is preventing things from happening.

I often meet people who ask me for help with their job search. Some are very senior. We talk about their CV/résumé and who else they could talk to. Then I ask them if they meditate. Some who don't meditate then decide to learn. It helps them to let go, so things can start happening.

Some already meditate but they still feel stuck, so we dig around to find out what they're holding onto. There's usually something they need to let go.

Another example is politics. Lots of people are angry about what's going on in the world. They're definitely not getting what they want – and the world carries on regardless. Sometimes we have to reach a state of exhaustion before we accept things as they are. Eventually we let go. We give up judging what's happening, or wanting to be right. We accept the situation and figure out what we can do to help. We stop complaining and start contributing. Then things change, often in ways we could never have anticipated.

What do you need to let go?

If you find yourself in a really difficult situation, it's time to step back and look at the big picture. Ask yourself this question: what do I need to let go? If you keep asking, you'll find the answer. Once you let go, the situation will change.

Maybe you'll move from one job, or business, or house, or city, or country, to another. Once we experience the benefits of letting go, it's a lot less scary. For some of us it's exciting.

Either you let go and create space, or life will create space for you

Some people who are fired from their jobs find a better job or start a successful business. They admit they would never have taken the risk of resigning from the old job. Life has created a space at the right time. In other cases, illness or bereavement makes them look at life in a new way. They become open to new ideas and things begin to change.

When you let go, what takes over?

As I said in the introduction, letting go is not the same as giving up or doing nothing. It simply means that we stop trying to control what happens. The obvious question is, <u>what</u> makes things happen?

The answer is beyond time and space, so it's pointless to name or describe it. That hasn't stopped people from trying. Here are twenty-eight examples, in alphabetical order:

- The Absolute
- Brahman (the ultimate reality underlying all phenomena)
- The cosmic energy
- The cosmic force of evolution
- The cosmos
- The Divine
- Divine energy
- Existence
- The flow of life
- God
- A higher power
- Infinite intelligence
- Life
- Life force
- Nature
- The Self (with a capital S, as opposed to the individual self, with a small s)
- The superabundant intelligence of the universe
- The Supreme Being
- The Tao (or Dao)
- 'That'
- That which is beyond name and form
- Unity
- The universal consciousness

- The universal energy
- The universal flow
- The universal force
- The universe
- The whole

When we let go, we acknowledge that our mind/brain/intellect doesn't have the answers. We create space. Things happen. Life unfolds naturally.

You aren't separate, so you don't need to control what's happening

For thousands of years it seemed to human beings that objects – including our bodies – were solid. Or at least the atoms that made up our bodies seemed solid enough. The word atom is derived from a Greek word that means *indivisible*. However, it turned out that atoms were made up of electrons, protons and neutrons. Then quantum mechanics demonstrated that not even sub-atomic particles are solid. For example, what we call an electron is simply a probability that an electron will appear. Electrons appear and disappear at random.

At the deepest level – which some of us experience during meditation – there is only pure consciousness, with no time or space, and therefore no separate objects. The more we experience pure consciousness, the more we realise that the perceived separation - between 'ourselves' and everything else - is an illusion. Here's a quotation which is often attributed to Albert Einstein:

"A human being is a part of the whole called by us universe, a part limited in time and space. He experiences himself, his thoughts and feelings as something separated from the rest, a kind of optical delusion of his consciousness.

CHAPTER 8

This delusion is a kind of prison for us, restricting us to our personal desires and to affection for a few persons nearest to us. Our task must be to free ourselves from this prison by widening our circle of compassion to embrace all living creatures and the whole of nature in its beauty."

Once we understand that we aren't separate, it's much easier to let go of the urge to control what happens. Everything is already being taken care of.

"For peace of mind, we need to resign as general manager of the universe."

Larry Eisenberg[1]

You can let go in any situation

Photography is another example of letting go. For me there are two main approaches. The first is to think about the picture I want to take and then set things up, as far as people and circumstances will allow. The second approach is to walk around holding my camera or mobile phone and see what happens.

The best photos almost always come from the second approach. Sometimes things align for a second or two – maybe only a split second – and the perfect composition appears on the memory card. I may not even see the final image on the screen or through the viewfinder. It goes straight from the scene in front of me to the memory card. It isn't John Purkiss who creates the image. The image simply appears.

(INSERT OTHER PEOPLE'S EXAMPLES.)

Let go of the urge to control conversations

Some of us try to control conversations by steering them in a certain direction, to make a point or pursue an agenda. Some try to control what's said, by labelling other people's comments inappropriate, racist, sexist, or whatever. Such conversations frequently achieve nothing.

It's better to let go and listen with an open mind. While you're listening you will notice thoughts and feelings that come up in reaction to what other people are saying. There may be labels or judgments. Just notice them and let them go. If you let go during conversations, you may notice some remarkable changes:

- You'll get on better with whoever you're listening to.
- Eventually, you may find yourself listening in what feels like an empty space, in which there are no separate people. There are just sounds and images which appear and disappear. Then there are thoughts and feelings which appear and disappear. You notice whatever comes up and let it go.
- You absorb lots of useful information.
- New ideas appear during the conversation.

You can still make your contribution, once the other person has finished speaking. It will appear naturally in the space.

Try showing up with no agenda

If someone invites me to a meeting, I frequently go with no agenda. I do my homework on whoever I'm going to meet, and the organisation where they work, but that's all. Then I listen very carefully to what they have to say, without interrupting or replying. When there's a space, things happen. In many cases, by the end of the meeting they're trying to figure out ways for us to work together.

This is how my friend Laurence Shorter describes his coaching work:

"When I'm coaching someone, I leave things open for chance. And I have found that when I am most relaxed, most unattached to any outcome whatsoever, that's when things go best. All of this requires me to be more interested in feeling relaxed than in creating value for the client. And when I can show up that way, value always comes. It's the paradox of all good work."

Let go of the urge to set deadlines
Some of us like to set deadlines. They can be useful. It can feel reassuring to have a time or a date by which something is supposed to happen. But if you can't predict the future, how on earth can you predict *when* something is going to happen?

It's OK to have an *idea* about when something is going to happen. But you'll create stress for yourself and others if you try to *force* it to happen by a certain time. Unexpected delays can turn out to be really helpful.

Think of an occasion when something you wanted to happen was delayed, and then worked out better than if it had happened 'on time'. Make a written note of it as a reminder.

If you're present and let go, there will be helpful coincidences
Many of us have noticed periods in our lives when everything seemed to flow naturally, without any major obstacles. If you're present and you let go, this may happen frequently. People appear at just the right time. Circumstances change. Things fall into place. It can feel uncanny and send a shiver down your spine.

Coincidence

You may have heard people say, "There are no coincidences". This is based on a linguistic misunderstanding. Coincidence simply means that two things happen at the same time.[2] It does not mean it's random or accidental. At the deepest level there's no separation: cause and effect are one. Things unfold, sometimes in ways that the mind struggles to comprehend or explain. But we don't need to worry about the mind. We can just meditate and let go.

- Let Go
- Create Space
- Things Happen

Embrace uncertainty

Many of us fear uncertainty. The financial markets certainly do. Whenever there's a crisis, some people react by selling their investments in a hurry

Even when there isn't a crisis, many of us try to remove uncertainty from our lives, in the hope of feeling 'safe' one day. The safety we're pursuing is a mirage. Any number of events could frustrate our attempts to be secure.

The more you practise the exercises in this book, the more comfortable with uncertainty you'll become. In the beginning you may see yourself as a separate individual trying to make your way through life. The more you let go of the thoughts and feelings that have been holding you back, the more you'll realise that you aren't separate.

9
Be Grateful and Let Go

Many of us focus on what we think is wrong or missing in our lives. Then we try to 'put things right'. In other words, we try to make reality conform to our ideas about how things should be. It's a recipe for stress and disappointment.

It's much better to appreciate whatever is happening now, and allow things to unfold naturally. (Please note that I will be using the words *appreciation* and *gratitude* interchangeably.)

Appreciate what is

My girlfriend at university was from Latin America. She had grown up during a conflict in which tens of thousands of people disappeared, including some of her sister's friends. For a while my girlfriend had been driven to school by a different route each day, with guns hidden under a blanket on the back seat of the car.

When I first met her parents, I was struck by the way they appreciated things, whether it was a daffodil or a place they'd visited. At first this seemed to me like escapism. Hadn't they seen all the poverty and conflict where they lived? I'd grown up on a diet of economic and social gloom served up by Radio Four every morning at breakfast time. However, none of my friends had been kidnapped or murdered.

Many years later, I began to understand how powerful their outlook was. Whether they did it consciously or not, they kept appreciating what was in front of them. Everything else faded into the background. My girlfriend's parents had married young and her father had worked his way up to become chairman of a large company. In the meantime they had brought up three children and now had several grandchildren. Appreciation worked for them.

You choose what you focus on

When I was twenty I had a habit of focusing on what I didn't like in each person or situation I encountered. Then I met people who focused on what they appreciated. This may sound naïve. Surely life is tough and we have to face reality. I agree that we face many challenges each day, but what we call reality is highly subjective. We're constantly choosing what we look at and how we look at it.

Photography illustrates this principle. When we take a photograph, we make lots of choices. To begin with, we choose to photograph one particular thing, rather than the thousands of other things we could have photographed. Then we choose what we're going to include in the frame and what we're going to exclude. We may zoom in or out before we take the picture. The aperture determines how much light we let into the lens, and how much of the picture is in focus. We can also change the colours using filters or electronic settings.

Every photograph is the product of dozens of choices. It can even include the choice not to choose carefully and to leave things to chance. I once read about a war photographer who used to set the automatic timer on his camera and then throw it in the air above his head. He got some interesting photographs that way – and survived the war.

Human beings are far more sophisticated than cameras. We choose what we look at and how we see things.

Try this:

Last thing at night, just before you go to bed, write down the five or six things you appreciate most about today. Exclude anything that happened before today or that might happen in the future. This exercise is purely about today. Here are some examples:

- *What you had for lunch*
- *Someone's positive reaction to some work you did for them*
- *A conversation you had with a friend*
- *The weather*
- *Some money you've received*
- *The project(s) you're working on*
- *A new experience you had today*
- *Something you've learned*
- *Something you've created.*

Once you've finished, go to bed. Notice how you feel as you do so. Notice how you feel when you wake up the next morning.

When I started practising this exercise I noticed that I went to bed feeling good. I used to feel a bit down in the mornings, but now I woke up feeling pretty good too. The way I felt about myself and my situation was gradually changing.

This exercise is based on facts: things that have already happened. All we're doing is changing what we focus on. Once we do so, we feel better and our lives begin to change.

Having learned this exercise, I experimented on my friends, as usual. One evening in December I had supper with a former colleague. She was living abroad and visiting London for a few days. Although we were good friends, she had a habit of complaining, which often left me feeling negative too.

We enjoyed our supper. When she asked me what I was doing, I told her about my latest experiments. This time it was the gratitude exercise. I explained to her how it worked.

After supper we went for a walk in Hyde Park. There was a German Christmas fair, with carrousels, wurlitzers and helter-skelters. We paused at a stand that sold large, leather-bound notebooks. She bought one and I thought nothing of it.

Two days later she returned home and sent me an email. The gratitude exercise was working. I've never seen anyone change so fast. She's been more positive ever since.

Some people do this exercise when they wake up, as well as when they go to bed. Both times are good, since the mind is relatively still. It makes it easier to change our mental habits.

Don't count your blessings

Many of us have been taught to 'count our blessings', but here's the danger: we start to believe that what we've accumulated is 'ours'. Then we cling to it and become afraid of losing it. A Buddhist text known as the *Dhammapada*[1] puts it like this:

" 'These are my sons. This is my wealth.' This is how the fool troubles himself. He doesn't even own himself, let alone his sons or his wealth."

You may be wondering what the difference is between being grateful and counting your blessings. Essentially:

- Being grateful happens moment by moment. You enjoy an experience and let it go.
- Counting your blessings involves labelling something as 'yours'. Then you suffer when it isn't yours any more. It could be a person, a possession, a reputation, some money...

It's better to enjoy each experience, be grateful for it, and let it go. For example, you might have a house in a nice neighbourhood, a loving family and lots of money. Any of them could disappear tomorrow. It's better to be grateful for each experience as it occurs, whether it's a smile from a child or a cup of tea on the lawn in the sunshine. Enjoy each experience and let it go.

Appreciate what's happening – and let it go

Once we acquire the habit of being grateful once or twice a day, it tends to spill over into the rest of our lives. We begin to appreciate everything. Try this:

As you go about your daily activities, keep bringing your attention back to the present. Notice the temperature of the room in which you're sitting. Notice the ground beneath your feet as you walk. Notice the sounds, the colours and the textures. Pay close attention to what people say, as well as how they say it.

Appreciate the air as it flows in and out of your body. Notice the weather and the physical sensations on your skin - and appreciate them. Appreciate the food you're eating, the people you're meeting, the ideas you're sharing, the work you're doing*, any money you're receiving and so on.

If you're delayed, notice how you feel about it. Notice the sensations within your body, which may include tension or irritation. Appreciate the opportunity to observe what's going on in your mind, your body and all around you. Appreciate the lessons you're learning.

*If you have no work right now, you can appreciate the opportunity to reflect and try new things.

At one point it was taking me a while to shift my focus from lack to appreciation, so I used an old trick to speed things up. I wrote the word **Appreciate!** in big, black letters on several large, fluorescent Post-It notes. Then I stuck them in various places, including on my desk, on the mirror above the sink and on the door of the refrigerator.

If you keep practising the exercises above you will start to feel different. Appreciation makes us happy. We can even be grateful when things *don't* go the way we wanted them to. We're learning a valuable lesson. It's just a question of looking closely to discover what that lesson is. It will have something to do with letting go.

Other people can help you see things in new ways

I have a friend who grew up in Iran during the eight-year war with Iraq. When she came to the UK she noticed that people complained about trains being dirty and late. She was grateful that there were trains.

Appreciation will improve your relationships

Many of us have tried to fix other people. It doesn't work. Focusing on what we don't like usually brings more of it. If we focus on what we appreciate in people, it can transform our relationships.

I'm not talking about flattery. I mean looking for what we appreciate most in people and focusing on that. It helps them to feel good about themselves. Some of them flourish as a result.

Be grateful for your intelligence, your energy and your ability to work hard

Some of us feel we have 'earned' what we have, through our intelligence and/or hard work. But where did your intelligence and ability to work hard come from? Weren't you given them also? In reality we've been given everything.

Be Present, Let Go, Be Grateful

Many of us do the following:

- Instead of being present, we worry about what's going to happen.
- Instead of letting go, we try to control what's happening.
- Instead of being grateful, we feel bad about all the things that don't seem to be happening.

You might call this *worrying, clinging and being resentful*. It hurts. It's better to *be present, let go and be grateful*. Try this:

As you go about your activities, keep returning to the present.

Place your attention on the breath as it flows in and out of your body. Pay attention to the colours, textures and shapes all around you. Pay attention to the sounds - nearby and far away.

Every time a thought comes, acknowledge it and let it go of its own accord. Bring your attention back to the present.

Let go of your hopes, dreams, concerns and worries. Shake your body whenever you have the opportunity. Stand up. Shake everything off.

Let go of your expectations. Be empty. Watch what happens, moment by moment, both inside you and all around you.

Be grateful for whatever happens. It could a sensation, such as a taste, a smell, a beautiful object, a fresh breeze or a sunset. Be grateful for everything you receive, however small. Don't judge it. Just be grateful.

When things don't happen, or are delayed, be grateful for anything that arises from it. Maybe there's a lesson to be learned. Watch how things unfold.

Be present and let go.

- **Let Go**
- **Create Space**
- **Things Happen**

10
Let Go, Be Curious

It's easy to judge whatever's happening as wrong. Then we disconnect ourselves from reality and become powerless. It's better to let go of judgments and be curious. Then we create space for new information, ideas and solutions.

Being open-minded takes effort

We might expect human beings to be open to information from any source, regardless of whether it fitted with their existing beliefs. Open-mindedness would help them to survive and prosper. But that's not the way things are. Most of us suffer from *confirmation bias*:

> **Confirmation bias** is the human tendency to look for information that confirms our beliefs and to ignore – or even fail to notice – evidence that contradicts them, if it's right in front of us. There's an extensive literature on confirmation bias in psychology, from contributors such as Daniel Kahneman[1], who won the Nobel Prize for economics.
>
> My friend Susanna Sällström Matthews teaches economics at Cambridge University. She says the origins of these biases are not yet fully understood: "Why are we biased against being open-minded? Why aren't we intrigued by evidence that contradicts our current beliefs, given the potential benefits from revising our beliefs to be a better match with the reality of our lives?"

However, there's also evidence that we can learn to overcome these biases and be more open-minded. The first step is to become aware of our confirmation bias. This is particularly relevant in the context of knowledge. Having acquired some knowledge we tend to see what's consistent with this knowledge instead of seeing the evidence that contradicts it. Knowledge can therefore make us more biased. Susanne suggests one technique for overcoming confirmation bias: let go of what you expect to find on the basis of your knowledge.

Many of us are trapped in a bubble

There's a natural human tendency to surround ourselves with friends and colleagues who agree with us. We then fall into the trap of believing that their opinions, tastes and behaviours are representative of the world at large. They aren't.

Social media have magnified this phenomenon, giving rise to *filter bubbles*:

A filter bubble occurs when the algorithm in a website uses information such as your location, past click behaviour and search history to guess what information you would like to see. The website then begins to serve you information which you'll like, and avoids serving you information which you probably won't like. As a result, the information you see will be different from the information that other people see. It's been tailored to your preferences. Over time, you will see less and less information that disagrees with your point of view.

On social media sites, you can accelerate this process by 'unfriending' anyone whose opinions you don't like. In due course, you will see little or no information which conflicts with your point of view. As a friend of mine put it, "How can this election result have happened? I don't know anyone who voted that way!"

Escaping from your bubble will help you spot new opportunities

Immediately after business school I spent three months working for Mercury Asset Management (MAM), which was Europe's largest independent fund management company. I quickly realised that I wasn't going to be a fund manager. However, I did learn a lot in a short period. I noticed that some of the most successful fund managers, at MAM and elsewhere, often read the 'tabloids' – the cheap, popular newspapers which have much larger circulations than the 'highbrow' newspapers. It was one way of discovering what people outside of their bubble were reading and thinking. It helped the fund managers to understand what was happening in the world around them. They had a much better sense of what was likely to happen next.

Try this:

- *Buy a newspaper or visit a news website that you wouldn't normally read, preferably one which isn't aimed at people of your occupation or social background.*

- *Go to a part of your city or region which you wouldn't normally visit (provided it's safe). Walk around. Watch and listen.*

- *Travel by public transport whenever possible. Put your phone away. Be present and pay attention to everything around you.*

- *When you meet someone whose opinion is different from yours, ask them lots of questions. Listen carefully. Learn as much as you can about what they're saying and how they see things.*

Letting go of your routine will help you to see a bigger picture. You will have new ideas and see new opportunities.

- **Let Go**
- **Create Space**
- **Things Happen**

11
Meditation Will Help You Let Go

All the meditation techniques in this book involve letting go

Some people say they've been meditating when they've been imagining or visualising something. Likewise, the word meditation is sometimes used to describe a practice involving words, sounds or music. This book is <u>not</u> about that. It <u>isn't</u> about filling your mind with thoughts, images or sounds.

All the meditation techniques described in this book involve letting go. There may be fewer and fewer thoughts. Sometimes there may be none.

You can 'meditate' everything you do

It's sometimes said that the ultimate meditation is to 'meditate' everything you do. When you open a door, you can place your attention on the texture and shape of the handle. When you walk, you can feel your feet pressing against the ground, and the temperature of the air against your skin. You can use any of your senses to return your attention to the present.

Put this book down and try this now. You can start by walking around slowly. Feel your feet pressing against the ground. Feel the breath flowing in and out of your body.

Every now and then you may notice that your attention has wandered. You may find yourself immersed in thoughts about the

past or the future, or what's happening somewhere else right now.
As soon as you notice this, bring your attention back to the present
by reconnecting with one of your senses. One way is to press your
thumbnails into your forefingers. A bit of discomfort can be useful.
It gets our attention.

When we bring our attention back to the present we return to
our natural state. Small babies often look us in the eye, with a
smile on their faces and no concerns about the past or the future.
With practice, we can be present more often.

Ideally, we'd alternate between (a) being present and (b)
thinking constructively. In reality, our minds still wander from
time to time. However, at least we now understand what's going
on. When we realise that our attention has wandered, all we need
to do is bring it gently back to the present, by placing it on our
breath or on one of our five senses. If we keep returning our
attention to the present, it gradually becomes a valuable habit.

If mindfulness doesn't work for you, try another technique

Some people find that mindfulness is the only meditation technique they need. It works for them and they don't need to look
elsewhere. I practised the techniques described in chapter 3 for
six years.

However, there are others who find that mindfulness is
hard work. Their attention keeps wandering and they have to
keep bringing it back. Instead of being able to let go, they find
themselves continually trying to control the mind.

If this happens to you, I suggest you consider other forms
of meditation:

Kindfulness

This is what Shamash Alidina has to say on the subject: "Mindfulness is about cultivating present moment awareness. But mindfulness can miss the heart of ancient eastern teachings: kindness and letting go. Renowned Buddhist monk Ajahn Brahm[1] coined the term *kindfulness* to highlight the importance of being kind to yourself and others." [2]

Yoga

In its traditional form, yoga *is* meditation. I'm not talking about 'beer yoga' or 'yoga to the music of Madonna'. I'm talking about yoga with traditional asanas (poses). You can usually tell they're traditional because they have Sanskrit names. Some people have made great progress in letting go through yoga.

> *Yoga* is a Sanskrit word meaning *union* or *connection*, and is related to the English work *yoke*. When most of us think of yoga we think of physical postures and breathing exercises. These are certainly part of the path of yoga, but it goes much deeper than that. When they're performed properly, they remove the impediments to the *inner experience* of the state of yoga. The state of yoga is experienced during meditation, which takes the awareness deep within, beyond thought. Another term for the state of yoga is *pure consciousness*, which I've used several times in this book. As it says in Patanjali's Yoga Sutra, "Yoga is the complete settling of the activity of the mind".[3]

Transcendental Meditation (TM)

TM was introduced to the West by Maharishi Mahesh Yogi[4]. The word *transcendental* may sound exotic, but transcending is something that millions of people have experienced. The Latin root of the verb *to transcend* means 'to move beyond'. During transcendence we move beyond the thinking process. Transcendence is *pure consciousness*, with no thoughts.[5]

As with mindfulness, the technique involves giving the mind something to do. In this case we use a *mantra* (a Sanskrit term meaning *mind instrument*[6]*).* The mantra is a word we use as a tool for meditation. We allow it to appear in the mind as gently as any other thought. Then we let go.

In TM you receive a personal mantra from your teacher. Then you begin to hear it over and over again in your mind, at least at the beginning of the meditation. All you have to do is *let the mantra come*. It begins to do its work automatically.

When I attended the introductory talk our teacher, Neil, explained that TM allows the mind to settle down, so the body settles down, providing deep rest. As a result, "the body is deeply rested. The mind is lively." He called this restful alertness.

The programme consisted of a few, short sessions. In between, we practised on our own. The first few times I found it difficult, but suddenly things began to happen. It felt like gentle electric pulses crossing my scalp from one side to the other. Then I learned to *let go* during meditation. They call it 'going deep'. It felt like dropping feet first into a deep pool while continuing to breathe normally. As Neil had predicted, there were times when the mantra dropped away, leaving me in a state of *no mind, no mantra*. It felt blissful.

One of the most striking aspects of TM was that it didn't require a big effort. Once I'd mastered the simple technique, it became easy. I also noticed that, when I didn't meditate for a day or so, I felt a bit stale. Once I'd meditated I felt refreshed. It was like a river that silted up and then began to flow again.

TM, like mindfulness, has well-documented health benefits. There are around 330 peer-reviewed studies of the biological and physiological effects of TM, and its benefits in many different conditions. At the most basic level, studies have shown that:

- TM increases brainwave coherence. It therefore strengthens communication between the brain's prefrontal cortex and other areas in the brain
- There is an increase in both alpha wave coherence (during wakeful relaxation) and beta wave coherence (during activity).

One of the best-known books on the subject was written by my friend Dr Norman Rosenthal[7], a world-renowned psychiatrist who conducted research at the National Institute of Mental Health in the USA for over 20 years. He was also the first to describe seasonal affective disorder (SAD) and develop light therapy as a means of treating it. In his book Transcendence[8], Norman describes how TM can be used to help people with high blood pressure, seasonal affective disorder, anxiety, depression, attention deficit disorder, addictions and post-traumatic stress disorder.

Strange as it may sound, a mantra can have a major effect on the mind and the body. Having learned the technique, I practised TM every day. Neil had suggested it was twice as efficient as sleep. If I was tired, it only took twenty minutes of TM for my brain to wake up again. It felt as though I'd slept for forty minutes to an hour.

I've since found that TM removes around 90% of the jet lag I used to experience. After learning TM I flew from London to Shanghai. It used to take up to four days for my body to adjust completely after a long-haul flight. As usual, I ate the meals they put in front of me and slept as much as I could. However, the big difference came when I was awake and unable to sleep. Whenever I was tired of reading I would stop and practise TM for twenty minutes. As a result, I arrived at my hotel in Shanghai relatively well rested. Then I slept for an hour or two. After that I was fine, with practically no jet lag. The same thing happened on my trip back to London.

Meditation will show you how connected everything is

As I explained earlier[9], the separation we perceive between ourselves and everything around us is an illusion. Despite this, most humans behave as though they were separate from each other.

I also told you how I learned mindfulness and then let go[10]. Shortly afterwards I moved from a failing business in one country to the perfect job in another. After I learned Transcendental Meditation there were further surprises.

I soon felt a stronger connection with people and with animals. Some animals demonstrate a very close connection with members of the same species. Maybe you've seen shoals of fish and flocks of birds that travel in dense formations and then turn in an instant, without bumping into each other. Usually, human beings are much less coordinated. However, we occasionally do something similar.

One day I had an unusual experience on a Tube train in London[11]. (I must warn you not to try this yourself.) I was casually dressed, on my way to a meeting with the founder of a software company. I was standing in one of the carriages, reading the news. Other people were standing or sitting. Some were chatting. Others were silent.

A black man, probably in his sixties, was sitting on one of the upholstered benches opposite a man of South Asian descent who looked around twenty. Every now and then the older man made a negative comment about the younger one. The younger one swore back at him, becoming angrier each time. I had a feeling the younger man was about to beat up the older one, in front of many other passengers. However, no one moved or said anything.

Within a few seconds, several of us were lying on top of the young Asian, who was flat on his face on his bench. I was closest to his right ear. I said, "Don't do anything. You'll go to jail."

A few seconds later, we all climbed off again – and went back to reading, etc. At the next stop he stood up, muttered something, and then stepped off the train and onto the platform. After he left, no one made any comment.

I've since described this episode to a friend who was in the army. He said I was mad. We could have been stabbed, etc. However, there was no thinking, communication or planning on our part. It happened in an instant.

Ideas and solutions come from *not* thinking
Have you ever done the following?

- You work on a problem until you get stuck and can't go any further.
- You do something physical such as walking, swimming or playing sport.
- The solution comes to you in a flash, either during the activity or shortly afterwards when you look at the problem again.

These experiences show us the power of not thinking. I first noticed it when I was working on mathematics problems at school. I've since experienced it in many other situations.

How about you?

When has a solution come to you after you stopped thinking and let go?

Write it down to remind yourself.

Meditation creates space for ideas and solutions

When I talked about meditation in chapter 3, I said that emptying the mind was an impossible task, at least initially. However, there are people who practise mindfulness consistently and sometimes experience periods when there are no thoughts. This is how Shamash Alidina describes it: "This emptying of the mind happens when the meditator stops trying to meditate. This letting go of control leads to a natural quieting of the mind over time. Just like the ripples in a lake dissipate if you stop touching the water."

Transcendental Meditation allows people to be conscious without any thoughts through the experience of transcendence. The mantra makes it happen. We let go and experience what Maharishi called 'unbounded awareness'.

Whichever technique you use, the important thing is to create a space in which ideas and solutions appear spontaneously. This is very useful for anyone who wants to do something new.

My friend Thomas Drewry is an entrepreneur and occasional stand-up comedian. Having practised TM for several years, he says that, "solutions and creative ideas often manifest themselves during or after meditation. All it takes is to be ready for the download."

Meditation and Science
Those who've been meditating for years know it works for them. Continuing scientific research provides further insights.

There are many meditation teachers with scientific backgrounds, including those mentioned in this book:

Name	Degree Subject
Ajahn Brahm	Theoretical physics
John Kabat-Zinn	Molecular biology
Maharishi Mahesh Yogi	Physics
Shamash Alidina	Chemical engineering

Albert Einstein talked about intuition and compassion, both of which are experienced by people who meditate regularly.

Don't forget your mental hygiene!
Whichever meditation technique you choose, make sure you do it every day. Skipping it feels like not taking a shower.

Meditation is the single most powerful tool for letting go and creating space.

- Let Go
- Create Space
- Things Happen

12
Letting Go in Action

You may be wondering why I've left this subject until now. The reason is that your actions will be far more effective if you've followed the previous steps described in this book.

Effective action is not the same as being busy

Western culture has a bias towards busyness. Doing nothing is often seen as bad. This has been ascribed to the Protestant work ethic, which the early settlers took with them from Europe to North America. In the seventeenth century the Massachusetts Bay Colony passed a law against idleness, stating that "No person, Householder or other shall spend his time idlely or unprofittably". [1]

Can you imagine? You're sitting on a park bench with your eyes closed. An idea for curing cancer begins to appear. Then you get arrested for idleness.

Some activity is counterproductive

Many of us rely on a fund manager to manage our pension or other investments. Every time s/he buys or sells a security there are transaction costs. The way to minimise these is to be disciplined in selecting securities and then hold them for long periods. What some fund managers do instead is buy and sell frequently in response to their changing ideas.

This hyperactivity leads to high transaction costs. Investors lose money. Many of them would be better off investing in a computerised index fund, instead of a fund managed by a human being.

Why do we take action that's unproductive?

Many of us keep busy in order to suppress painful memories and emotions. However:

- Painful memories still cause us to react, like a football held deep underwater which suddenly rises to the surface.
- Painful emotions affect our thoughts and actions, which are far less productive than they could be. Sometime the results are the opposite of what we want.

The exercises in chapter 7 will help you remove painful memories and emotions. If you haven't completed them yet, please go back and do so before you take any action. Action based on pain leads to more pain. Here are some examples:

- Starting a relationship because you feel lonely
- Attacking someone (verbally or physically) because you feel threatened
- Taking a job or assignment because you're afraid of poverty

The mind can't figure out the best course of action

You may recall this sentence from chapter 2: "The mind cannot rise above what it already knows". To put it another way, the intellect can't figure out the best course of action based on existing information.

Conventional economics assumes that we all act rationally in our best interests. Behavioural economics has shown that we often don't. Even in the cases where we do act rationally, our actions have far-reaching effects, many of which we can't anticipate. We keep taking action without knowing what the effects will be. We get frustrated when things don't work out the way we want. Sometimes there are unintended side effects which cause us to suffer. We may also feel regret when we cause harm to others.

If the mind can't figure out the right course of action, what's the solution? The answer is *spontaneous right action.*

Spontaneous right action is when someone only acts in ways that are ideal for the welfare of all beings. This happens when his or her consciousness aligns with that which is beyond name and form (for which I provided 28 names in chapter 8). You realise you aren't just a brain and a body trying to force your way through life. Instead, you're aligned with the source of everything. Your actions are in accord with nature.

The way to align yourself is to meditate every day. One sign that it's starting to work is that your intuition becomes stronger.

Steve Jobs, the founder of Apple, practised Zen meditation for many years. This is what he told his biographer, Walter Isaacson: "If you just sit and observe, you will see how restless your mind is. If you try to calm it, it only makes things worse, but over time it does calm, and when it does, there's room to hear more subtle things — that's when your intuition starts to blossom and you start to see things more clearly and be in the present more. Your mind just slows down, and you see a tremendous expanse in the moment. You see so much more than you could see before. It's a discipline; you have to practice it." [2]

Intuition is widely misunderstood. Some people regard it as 'fuzzy thinking' or 'lazy thinking'. In fact, intuition comes from *not* thinking. Intuition is 'insight without reasoning'. It happens in a flash.

Western culture places a big emphasis on *analysis*, whose Greek root means *loosening* or *breaking up*. We break a problem up into small pieces in order to understand and solve it. Many academic and professional disciplines are based on analysis, including logic, mathematics, economics, law, medicine, engineering and science.

Sometimes analysis is *not* the right tool for the job, but we persist in applying it. To paraphrase Mark Twain[3], to a person with a hammer, everything looks like a nail.

Analysis and intuition are both useful

Here's an alternative way of looking at analysis versus intuition:

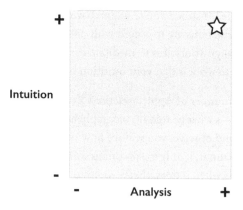

The star in the top right-hand corner is the sweet spot: the ideal combination of analysis and intuition. Education and training can help us to develop analytical skills. Meditation strengthens our intuition.

Too much analysis can weaken your intuition

Many of us are intuitive as children, but become less so during our education, training and work experience.

Having studied languages, economics, accounting, finance, strategy and so on, I became very good at analysis. I had the certificates to prove it. But when I developed an interest in executive search – otherwise known as headhunting – I suddenly realised that I was unable to 'read' people. In other words, I didn't understand them intuitively when I met them. One of my friends at business school clearly did have plenty of intuition. While I'd been analysing companies and markets, he'd been an Inspector in the Hong Kong Police and had worked for the Foreign Office in Nigeria.

For me, the big change came when I learned to meditate. I kept bringing my attention back to the present several times each day. I noticed that the more I practised being present, the stronger my intuition became. At first it felt like being a child again. I would simply have a feeling about someone or something. As the thoughts began to die down, everything became clearer.

Suddenly I began to understand myself much better. I also realised that I could now 'read' other people. I knew I was ready to recruit senior executives and board members.

Intuition is also very valuable in our social lives. If we pay attention to our intuition when we're with people, we can save ourselves a lot of time and trouble.

Analysis and intuition complement each other
There's a common misconception that 'analytical people' and 'intuitive people' are at opposite ends of a spectrum. However, some of us use both. One example was John Viney[4], the Chairman - Europe of Heidrick & Struggles, who taught me a great deal about executive search. John had a very strong intellect, which he'd used to gain a PhD in astrophysics at Cambridge while completing a masters degree in music. However, he was also

highly intuitive. When we were discussing whether a candidate would fit with a particular client, he would often ask, "Can you see them together?" The answer was either yes or no. His question was directed to the intuition. If I tried to analyse the situation, he would say, "No. Can you *see* them together?"

You can make better decisions by combining analysis and intuition

These are the steps:

1. Analyse the situation, so you understand it intellectually.
2. Do something to let go. Meditate, go for a walk, go swimming…
3. Use your intuition to make decisions. Do what <u>feels</u> right.

One example is when you recruit someone, for your organisation or any other. You can read candidates' CVs/résumés and gather data online, which you then analyse. But you should also use your intuition. When you meet each person, you may have a feeling about whether they're right for the organisation. Pay attention to that feeling.

Find the meditation technique that works for you

If you've been meditating for a while but don't recognise the benefits I'm describing in this book, I suggest you review your meditation technique. Ask your teacher to check it for you. If that doesn't work, it may be time to try a new approach. Meditation has such a profound effect on our lives that it's worth making the effort to get it right.

Every action you take will come back to you in some form

Most people have heard of the law of karma. (*Karma* is a Sanskrit word which means *action*.) Simply put, it says that whatever action you take will come back to you in some form. It's like throwing a stone into the centre of a pond. The ripples radiate from the centre to the sides. Then they bounce back towards the centre.

The effect of each action always returns to us. We just don't know when or how. Sometimes it's surprisingly quick.

A year after I left Heidrick & Struggles, my new executive search business ground to a halt. The UK was in the midst of a recession and I had no search assignments. Then I received a phone call from INSEAD's alumni association. Large numbers of its MBA graduates had either lost their jobs or expected to do so shortly. Could I come and give a talk about how to get a job via headhunters?

I felt a bit of a fraud, since I had no work either, but I also had a feeling I should help. I let go of my concerns about my own predicament, put together a PowerPoint presentation and went to the event. There were around 75 people in the audience who either had no job or expected to be fired in the near future. I did my best to explain how executive search works, how to get onto a short list and how they could maximise their chances of being offered a job.

On the stage beside me was an executive from a large company. He spoke next, explaining how firms like his recruited new staff. Part way through his presentation, he said he'd been struggling to recruit a group treasurer for several months, so he would talk to me afterwards. My colleagues and I soon began work on a search assignment for him, which went very well. Then his company gave us a second, more senior assignment. They became a big client of ours.

That summer I started turning the PowerPoint presentation into a rough draft of a book, which I wrote with Barbara Edlmair.

A friend introduced us to a publisher, who quickly made an offer for it. *How To Be Headhunted*[5] was published a few months later. If you've ever been involved in publishing, you'll know it rarely goes that smoothly.

Be authentic. Say what you think and how you feel

I stopped eating meat when I was 25. Every now and then someone asks me why. It's usually when we're eating together. Not wanting to be antisocial, my response for years was, "I'll tell you another time". I never did.

I became less and less comfortable with this approach. I was promising to do something and not doing it. I was shying away from saying how I felt about something important. It felt *inauthentic.*

Eventually a solution occurred to me, and I've used it ever since. If someone asks me why I don't eat meat, I say "For every reason". It feels much better. If they want to find out what that means, there's an abundance of free information on the internet.

Are there any topics on which you shy away from saying what you think or how you feel? Write them down now.

Writing down the issues you've suppressed in your conversations with other people can bring up all kinds of fears. What if they get angry with me? What if they leave me? What if I lose a customer? And so on.

As usual, you have a choice. You can either suppress those fears or face up to them. The sofa exercise on page 50 will help you do the latter. Then they'll start to lose their power over you.

I'm not suggesting you go around broadcasting your opinions, face-to-face or online. I *am* suggesting you give people a straight answer when they ask you what you think or how you feel.

That's how the world changes. Gradually, more and more people become aware. Eventually it reaches the point where something is done about it. Society moves forwards. But it won't happen if you and I don't say what we think or feel when we're asked. I recommend these six steps, which draw on earlier chapters:

1. Be curious. Gather lots of information about what's going on around you.

2. Be open. Let go of labels, judgments, conclusions, fantasies and the need to be right.

3. Meditate. Your intuition will grow. You'll see things that other people have missed.

4. Analyse the situation. Form an initial hypothesis.

5. Update your hypothesis as you gather more information. Let go of any attachment to knowing or being right.

6. Ask other people what they think or feel on a particular topic. Learn as much as you can from them.

These six steps will help you to make a valuable contribution. If someone asks your opinion, you can tell them. They can use the information as they see fit. You're also likely to feel better now that you're no longer hiding your thoughts or feelings. (I felt lighter, as though I'd let go of some burden.) Other people may see things differently from you. That's fine.

You don't need to be dogmatic. You can just say "I have a feeling that..." or "I am concerned about...". It's very hard for anyone to attack us if we simply describe our thoughts and feelings. All we're doing is describing what's happening.

If you do this, you're likely to feel better and learn a lot. Your relationships may also improve as you and the people around you understand each other better.

The more we let go of thoughts and feelings, the freer we are to explore and learn. We gather useful information. We become more aware of what's happening. We're more likely to notice the opportunities in front of us.

Allow people to come and go

As you become more authentic, you'll notice changes in the people around you. Some will behave differently towards you. Others will go away and be replaced by new people. This may feel unsettling at first. However, things will happen much more easily with people who are on the same wavelength as you.

Allow everything to come and go

One of the most common sources of pain is clinging to possessions and experiences, which naturally come and go. Everything that belongs to you will one day cease to exist or belong to someone else. It's best to let go and enjoy the moment.

Let go of the person in your stories

This may sound weird at first, but bear with me. Remember the stories we talked about in chapter 2? I hope the chapters that followed have helped you to drop most or all of them. But what about the *person* who appeared in those stories? Sooner or later we can let go of him or her too.

When we're born we simply *are*. As small babies we have experiences, we laugh and we cry. But we don't yet have a story about ourselves as a person. That comes later.

We're given a name, a mother tongue, a nationality and perhaps a religion. Over the years that follow, our parents, teachers, bosses and others keep telling us that John Purkiss or Freda Smith (or whoever) has been naughty or nice, has a great future (or not), and so on. It's one huge story, which is constantly being added to. By the time you're an adult, you've accumulated lots of episodes describing the past adventures, achievements and sufferings of John or Freda.

Eventually you may realise that the story of John or Freda is just a stream of repetitive thoughts. The story may seem real – like watching a film – but it isn't. It's just a series of thoughts strung together.

So what's the alternative? What if you aren't the person in the story? Who are you? The answer is that you simply *are*. You're the pure awareness or pure consciousness that you experience sometimes during meditation. It's the same when you're seven as when you're seventy. Thoughts, emotions and sensations appear and disappear within that consciousness or awareness.

Letting go of the person may sound scary at first. But once you get used to it, it's liberating and exciting. Everything happens in awareness. You no longer need to deal with John or Freda and their stories. Life becomes an exciting adventure that's unfolding. You may also find yourself laughing more.

Everything happens more smoothly and easily. There's no John or Freda to get in the way. There's only a vast, empty space in which things happen:

You can start doing this now:

Keep your eyes open.

Place your attention on the breath as it flows in and out.

Listen as far as possible into the distance – beyond the sounds nearby.

Now bring your attention back to your immediate surroundings.

Notice the sounds, images and sensations as they appear and disappear.

Keep bringing your attention back to the present. Feel the empty space.

Observe what's happening in your body and all around you.

Allow your body to take whatever action feels appropriate.

Observe your body as it takes action - or remains still.

Keep doing this.

Remember:

- **Let Go**
- **Create Space**
- **Things Happen**

Conclusion

In the Introduction I told you what life would be like after letting go. If you've done the exercises in this book, you're likely to have noticed some of those changes taking place already.

Now I can tell you how this all fits together:

1. The more we let go, the more we create space for things to happen. We let go of the urge to control and stop trying to solve every problem using our brains.

2. The most powerful tool for letting go is daily (silent) meditation. It helps us to experience pure consciousness – a limitless space in which creative ideas and solutions appear.

3. What makes things happen is infinitely intelligent, and beyond name and form. We tune into it during pure consciousness, which gradually spreads from meditation to the rest of our lives.*

4. Meditation also helps us to observe our thoughts and see what we need to let go.

5. The people you find most annoying will show you what you need to embrace and let go.

6. We need to let go of painful experiences, so they no longer shape the future.

7. Gratitude helps us to let go. The better we feel, the more easily things happen.

*Right now I'm completing the TM-Sidhi Programme, which teaches meditators to think and act from pure consciousness.

8. Curiosity helps us to tune into what's happening, without judging or labelling. Then we can play our part.

9. The natural result of all this is *spontaneous right action*: we only act in ways that are ideal for the welfare of all beings. It's the most fulfilling way to live.

10. The final step is to let go completely, as I will explain in the Epilogue. Things happen easily, with little or no stress. Life is more fulfilling than ever before.

Epilogue

Essentially, we face a choice between:
a) Trying to achieve everything through mental and physical effort, and
b) Letting go, allowing that which is beyond name and form to do everything.

I hope you've completed the exercises. If so, you're likely to have discovered for yourself that letting go allows things to happen much more easily.

I've done my best to minimise the number of metaphors in this book. However, I would now like to introduce a new one which helps us to understand what we've been experiencing.

Approach (a) above can work pretty well for years, maybe even a few decades. But at some point it doesn't work any more. Sooner or later we run into a wall, or rather, what *seems* like a wall. At this point many of us get frustrated, angry and/or depressed. We can't go any further. We feel stuck. Life is terrible.

Eventually, some of us realise that it isn't a wall. It's a big step. In order to continue moving forwards, we have to go up a level:

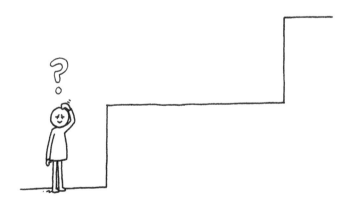

In my case, it felt as though I was running along a flat surface. Then, all of a sudden, I hit a wall. My existing approach didn't work any more. Eventually it dawned on me that this was another step upwards. I needed to let go of something in order to go up a level. Once I figured out what it was, I moved up to another flat surface and kept moving forwards, maybe for several months or a year or two, until I hit another wall. And so it continued, up a long flight of steps. The higher we go, the clearer things become. We feel better and things happen more easily.

This process of moving up from one level to another is about *letting go*, not acquiring. We let go of judgments, labels, attachments, painful memories, mental patterns, preconceptions and so on. The more we let go, the more we enjoy life and the more easily things happen.

Let go *completely*

Now it's time for a very important step, which is sometimes called *Surrender*. Many people find this word scary, which is why I haven't used it for any of the chapter headings or sub-headings. (Sneaky, eh?) Allow me to explain.

Several times, my life has been changed by a few words in a book. I hope you've had a similar experience while reading this one. Anyway, one day I was reading Swamiji's commentary on chapter 18 of the *Bhagavad Gita*[1], one of the most important texts in the *Vedas*. The chapter heading in his commentary is *Drop Everything and Surrender*. Two sentences jumped out at me:

"You need not renounce what you already have. All you need to do to achieve happiness is to renounce what you *do not* have."[2]

These sentences stuck in my mind. It was clear to me that I *hadn't* done this. I was still trying to achieve various goals, in some cases with no visible success. Having been brought up as a Christian, I was also praying for things to happen – which in many cases they weren't.

A few days later I had a cup of tea with a friend. Her life had changed fast in the last few months, and she'd just got married. She told me two things:

- "I didn't trust life. I used to worry a lot."
- "Then I realised that life was supporting me exactly as I was."

Does this ring a bell for you? It did for me:

- Despite everything I'd learned, I still worried about how things would turn out.
- My religious upbringing definitely *did not* suggest that life would support me exactly as I was. On the contrary, I was heading for disaster unless I did A, B and C.

How about you?

- Do you trust life, or do you worry about what will happen?
- Do you feel that life supports you exactly as you are?

At this point I realised that I needed to let go completely. In other words, it was time to *surrender.* Maybe it's time for you to do the same. Here are the steps:

1. Forget about your desires, goals, plans, dreams and expectations. Imagine yourself throwing them all away.
2. Now do whatever feels appropriate, moment by moment*. Follow your intuition. Sometimes there may be lots of action. Sometimes there may be none.
3. Let go of any thoughts about the outcome. Don't bother thinking about results. Just immerse yourself in whatever you're doing and enjoy it.

* If you keep a to-do list, pick the item which needs your attention now and work on it.

So I carried out the three steps described above. (Point 1 included no longer praying for X or Y to happen in my life. I prayed for people who were suffering to be healed. That was all.) This is what happened:

- I suddenly felt more relaxed.
- I began to notice my surroundings in more detail. (Walking down the street where I'd lived for eight years, I noticed for the first time that the houses at the end of the street had attic windows.)
- I was present most of the time, and it was effortless.
- Colours seemed a lot brighter.
- I went for a walk and the solution to a tricky business problem appeared when I wasn't thinking about it.
- I became much more productive, whether I was writing a document, organising something or communicating.
- I had more energy and started exercising more.
- I found myself enjoying life moment by moment, without any expectations.
- I felt grateful for everything that was happening.
- I had a strong feeling of love. (There's no other word for it.)
- I was much less irritated by what I saw happening around me. Instead, I found myself laughing more – including at myself.

So the final step – at the top of the staircase – is *surrender:* we let go *completely*. We allow that which is beyond name and form to do everything. We no longer need to figure it all out intellectually. We relax and enjoy life while one thing happens after another. Of course I still lapse into the old way now and then. I catch myself trying to 'achieve' things through mental and physical effort. But it's painful, which wakes me up. Then I remember that John Purkiss is just a story. I'm much more than that.

I encourage you to let go completely and experience this for yourself. Let me know how you get on! You're welcome to share your experiences of letting go at:

http://facebook.com/groups/thepoweroflettinggo

References

Introduction

1. www.insead.eu
2. Sir Karl Popper (1902 – 1994) is regarded as one of the greatest philosophers of science of the 20th century. He argued in favour of *empirical falsification*: while a theory can never be proven, experiments can show it to be false.

Chapter 2: Start Letting Go of Your Stories

1. With David Royston-Lee: www.brandyou.info
2. Carl Jung (1975 – 1961)
3. *A Rich Man's Secret*, Llewellyn Publications (ISBN: 978-1567185805)

Chapter 3: Stand Back and Observe Thoughts as They Come and Go

1. See Recommended Reading.
2. See Recommended Reading.
3. John Kabat-Zinn (born 1944)
4. Thich Nhat Hanh (born 1926)

Chapter 4: A Whole Load of Things You Can Let Go

1. www.myersbriggs.org
2. *Hamlet*, Act 2, Scene 2.
3. The expression "Sai Weng Shi Ma" 塞翁失馬 is a Chengyu, or traditional Chinese idiomatic expression. Chengyu were widely used in Classical Chinese and are still common in the modern spoken and written language.
4. www.dariusnorell.com
5. Latin: *con-* means *completely. Claudere* means *to shut.*

6. *Tao Te Ching*, by Lao Tsu. Translated by Gia-Fu Feng and Jane English.
7. Sir John Templeton (1912 – 2008)
8. Nicholas Taleb, *The Black Swan – The Impact of the Highly Improbable*
9. Woody Allen (born 1935)

Chapter 5: Let Go of Suffering

1. I learned this technique from Dr David R. Hawkins. See *Letting Go – The Pathway of Surrender*, listed under Recommended Reading.

Chapter 6: Discover What Else You Need to Let Go

1. German: "Ich will lieber ganz sein als gut!"
2. German: "Alles was uns an anderen missfällt, kann uns zu besserer Selbsterkenntnis führen."
3. This metaphor appears in John Welwood's book, *Love and Awakening ("Loss of Being: Closing down the Palace",* pages 11-14). Debbie Ford also uses it in *The Dark Side of the Light Chasers* (listed under Recommended Reading).

Chapter 7: Let Go of the Past

1. Neuro-linguistic programming (NLP) was created by Richard Bandler and John Grinder in California, USA in the 1970s.
2. Norman E. Rosenthal, M.D., *The Gift of Adversity*, page 233.
3. www.nithyananda.org
4. Paramahamsa Nithyananda, YouTube, May 2, 2013. www.nithyananda.org
5. The completion technique is known as *swapoornatva kriya* in Sanskrit. *Swa-* means *self* (like *soi* in French). *Poornatva* (also spelt *purnatva*) means *fullness* or *perfection*. *Kriya* means *action,*

deed, or *effort*. The *swapoornatva kriya* is the twenty-second technique in *Vijñāna Bhairava Tantra*: "Look at your past, disidentified; let attention be at a place where you are seeing some past happening; and even your form having lost its present characteristics is transformed." Swamiji explains all of this at **http://nithyanananda.org**. (Type *swapoornatva kriya* into the search box.)

6. See Recommended Reading

Chapter 8: Let Go of the Urge to Control

1. Larry Eisenberg (born 1919)
2. Medieval Latin: *co-* means *together with*. *Incidere* means *to fall upon* or *to fall into*.

Chapter 9: Be Grateful and Let Go

1. *The Dhammapada*, Chapter 5 – *The Fool*, verse 62. Translated by Juan Mascaró. (Penguin Classics, 1973. ISBN: 0-14-044284-7)

Chapter 10: Let Go, Be Curious

1. Daniel Kahneman (born 1934)
   See Recommended Reading, page 134

Chapter 11: Meditation Will Help You Let Go

1. Ajahn Brahm (born 1951). See Recommended Reading
2. You can try Shamash's online programme at www.kindfulnessonline.com. The first seven days are free.
3. Patanjali, *Yoga Sutra*, chapter 1, verse 2, translated by Maharishi Mahesh Yogi
4. Maharishi Mahesh Yogi (1918 – 2008)
5. The Sanskrit term for transcendence (pure consciousness) is *turiya chetana*. *Turiya* means *fourth*. (The first three states of consciousness are waking, dreaming and sleeping.)

6. The Sansrkit word *mantra* consists of *man*, which means *think,* and the suffix *tr*, which means *tool* or *instrument.*
7. www.normanrosenthal.com
8. See Recommended Reading.
9. Chapter 8, page 80.
10. Chapter 2, pages 10 to 14.
11. The Tube is a popular term for the London Underground, a public mass transit system.

Chapter 12: Letting Go in Action

1. General Court, Massachusetts Bay Colony, 1633.
2. *Steve Jobs*, by Walter Isaacson
3. Mark Twain (1835 – 1910)
4. Dr John Viney (1947 – 2009)
5. *How to be Headhunted*, by John Purkiss and Barbara Edlmair. (How To Books, 2005)

Epilogue

1. *Bhaghavad Gita* (Sanskrit) means Song of the Lord.
2. *Bhaghavad Gita Demystified*, by Nithyananda, volume 3, page 443. This book has been reproduced as a free download entitled *Drop Everything and Surrender,* which is available from www.nithyananda.org. See Recommended Reading. This quotation is on page 33 of the download.

Recommended Reading

On Letting Go of Your Story

- *Loving What Is: Four Questions That Can Change Your Life*, by Byron Katie, with Stephen Mitchell
  Byron Katie "discovered that when I believed my thoughts, I suffered, but that when I didn't believe them, I didn't suffer, and that this is true for every human being". She explains how to do 'The Work', which relieves this suffering.

- *Who Would You Be without Your Story? – Dialogues with Byron Katie.*
  This book is a series of 15 dialogues with audience members who are doing 'The Work'. Having seen Byron Katie live, I can confirm how effective her teaching method is. You can download what you need to get started at www.thework.com.

On Being Present

- *The Power of Now: A Guide to Spiritual Enlightenment*, by Eckhart Tolle
  This is one of the best-known books on being present. At the age of 29 Eckhart had a profound experience that led him to write *The Power of Now*. It draws on several traditions to describe a belief system based on living in the present.

- *Practising the Power of Now*, by Eckhart Tolle
  This is a collection of extracts from *The Power of Now* (described above) which was published in the UK in 2001. If you're new to Eckhart Tolle's work, you may wish to start with this book which is shorter and clearer.

On Mindfulness, Kindfulness and Zen

- *Mindfulness for Dummies*, by Shamash Alidina
  Shamash has attended retreats with Jon Kabat-Zinn, the Dalai Lama, Matthieu Ricard and Thich Nhat Hanh. Shamash is now one of the UK's best-known mindfulness teachers. This is the first of his books on the subject.

- *Kindfulness*, by Ajahn Brahm
  (INSERT TEXT)

- *Zen Mind, Beginner's Mind – Informal talks on Zen meditation and practice*, by Shunryu Suzuki
  Suzuki was a respected Zen master in Japan when he moved to the United States in 1958. He became one of the most influential Zen teachers of his time. This book will appeal to practitioners of *any* form of meditation – not just Zen.

On Being Present While Thoughts Come and Go

- *The Inner Game of Tennis*, by W. Timothy Gallwey
  Timothy Gallwey learned to meditate and found his tennis improved. The 'inner game' is played against opponents such as nervousness and self-doubt. Peak performance occurs when the mind is still and at one with what the body is doing. His later books include *Inner Skiing* and *The Inner Game of Golf.*

On the Shadow / Dark Side

- *The Dark Side of the Light Chasers*, by Debbie Ford
  We try to be good. In other words, we 'chase the light'. In the process we repress many aspects of ourselves, which become part of our *dark side*, otherwise known as the *shadow*. Debbie shows how to reintegrate your shadow and become whole.

On Letting Go of the Urge to Control

- *Tao Te Ching*, by Lao Tsu, translated by Gia-Fu Feng and Jane English
  This is an excellent English translation of the *Tao Te Ching*, which dates back to at least the fourth century BC and is normally attributed to Lao Tsu ("old master"), a record-keeper at the Zhou Dynasty court. An enjoyable read.

- *The Lazy Guru's Guide to Life*, by Laurence Shorter
  The author and illustrator have distilled some of the great wisdom traditions into a few pages of entertaining text and cartoons. There's a simple, powerful exercise in three steps. I read it in under an hour, and put it into practice right away.

On the Illusion of Separation

- **Beyond Knowledge**, by Jean Klein and Emma Edwards
  Jean Klein was a philosopher of Advaita Vedanta, who taught students to open themselves to their "true nature: the 'I am' of pure consciousness." He emphasised the direct way to knowledge, without elaborate programmes or practices.

- *Good Company*, by His Holiness Shantanand Saraswati
  Shantananda Saraswati taught the philosophy of Advaita, usually translated as "non-duality", "not two", or "one without a second". *Good Company* is an anthology of 40 of his talks recorded between 1961 and 1985.

- *The Upanishads*, by Vernon Katz and Thomas Egenes
  An accessible translation of a very important text. The *Upanishads* are also known as the *Vedanta*, meaning the end of the *Veda*, or knowledge. The 20-page introduction explains the context and principal themes.

- ***Wholeness and the Implicate Order***, David Bohm
  David Bohm was a renowned physicist whose work was
  influenced by Albert Einstein, Krishnamurti and the Dalai
  Lama. In this book he develops "a theory of quantum physics
  which treats the totality of existence as an unbroken whole".

On Letting Go of Suffering

- ***Letting Go – The Pathway of Surrender***, by David R.
  Hawkins, MD, PhD
  David Hawkins was a psychiatrist and researcher who
  developed a simple and effective means of removing the inner
  blocks to happiness. He describes it in chapter 2 of this book
  under the heading, *The Mechanism of Letting Go*.

On Behavioural Economics

- ***Thinking, Fast and Slow***, by Daniel Kahneman
  Conventional economics assumes that human beings are
  rational. Psychologist Daniel Kahneman demonstrates that
  they frequently are not. The appendices present the ideas
  cited by the committee that awarded him the Nobel Prize.

On Transcendental Meditation

- ***Catching the Big Fish – Meditation, Consciousness, and
  Creativity***, by David Lynch.
  David Lynch is a film-maker whose work includes *The
  Elephant Man*, *Mulholland Drive* and *Blue Velvet*. This book
  describes how transcendence enables us to experience pure
  consciousness and creativity. Beautifully written.

- *Science of Being and Art of Living: Transcendental Meditation*, by Maharishi Mahesh Yogi
In this book Maharishi introduces the technique of Transcendental Meditation (TM), which comes from the ancient Vedic tradition (as do yoga and Ayurvedic medicine). It will make most sense to readers who have already learned TM.

- *Transcendence: Healing and Transformation Through Transcendental Meditation*, by Dr Norman E. Rosenthal
Norman is a clinical professor of psychiatry. *Transcendence* is one of the best-known books on TM. It combines scientific evidence, case studies and interviews with Paul McCartney, Russell Brand, David Lynch and others.

On Enlightenment

- *Be As You Are: The Teachings of Sri Ramana Maharshi*
Ramana Maharshi lost his sense of an individual identity at the age of 16. He taught that self-realisation – or enlightenment – is a natural condition for human beings, and can be discovered through the process of *self-inquiry* described in these talks.

- *Breath of the Absolute – Dialogues with Mooji*
Mooji was born in Jamaica and moved to London at the age of 15. He is now based in Portugal and travels extensively, teaching *self-inquiry* in the tradition of Sri Ramana Maharshi (see above). The dialogues in this book took place in Tiruvannamalai, India.

- *Living Enlightenment*, by Paramahamsa Nithyananda
Sri Nithyananda Swami is a guru within the Hindu tradition. His ashram is located near Bangalore, India. This 800-page book covers a wide range of topics in detail, with clear explanations of Sanskrit terms.

On Career Management

- ***How to Be Headhunted – The Insider's Guide to Making Executive Search Work for You***, by John Purkiss and Barbara Edlmair
  Headhunting – or *executive search* – has long been shrouded in mystique. This book helps readers to market themselves to executive search consultants and be included on short lists for the senior jobs that interest them most.

- ***Brand You***, by John Purkiss and David Royston-Lee
  Brand You shows how to build a personal brand based on your talents, values and purpose. It then uses archetypes to help readers create a powerful brand identity which they can communicate both on- and offline.

On Surrender

- ***The Surrender Experiment***, by Michael A. Singer
  Mickey Singer was a doctoral student in economics when he learned to meditate. This led to a profound spiritual experience. He decided to surrender to life – and let go of self-centred thoughts and emotions. The results were extraordinary.

- ***Drop Everything and Surrender***,
  by Paramahamsa Nithyananda
  You can download this book as a PDF free of charge from www.nithyananda.org, either via this link (books.nithyananda.org/product/**drop-everything-surrender/**) or by entering the title into the search box. On page 82 he says, "Surrender itself is enlightenment. At that moment you experience the Truth."

Acknowledgements

I would like to thank the following, in addition to those already named in the text:

- Jacq Burns, my writing coach and agent, for her continuous feedback through many drafts.
- Neil Lukover for teaching me Transcendental Meditation.
- Shamash Alidina and Dr Norman Rosenthal for advising me on mindfulness and Transcendental Meditation respectively, and allowing me to quote from their work.
- Nell Axelrod and Ping Xu for advising me on the Chinese proverb in chapter 4.
- Mali Mizrahi and Marcus Weston for teaching me at the Kabbalah Centre.
- Ivana Sretenovic and Mahant Ma Nithya Atmadayanda for introducing me to Paramahamsa Nithyananda.
- Irene Brankin, David Royston-Lee and Adina Tarry for their advice on psychology.
- Dr Susanna Sällström Matthews for her advice on economics and the scientific method.
- Jeremy Marshall for his critique of the text from a Christian point of view.
- Susanne Worsfold for the layout and design of the text.
- Jim Shannon for the cover design.
- Ben Gold for the portrait photograph on the back cover.
- Rose Alexander for her advice on intellectual property law.

I am very grateful to everyone who has read various drafts and given me their feedback, or had ideas which have helped to make this book better. I apologise to anyone I have omitted; please contact me and I will include you in the next edition.

In the meantime I would like to thank Anthony Abis, Shamash Alidina, Gavin Andrews, Dr Afzana Anwer, Robert Ashdown, Nell Axelrod, André Berry, Patricia Bidi, Emma Bondor, Paul Bramley, Pierce Casey, Marion Chalmers, Charles Cooper, Sara Cooper, David Coulson, Julie Cross, Thomas Drewry, David Dwek, Dr Barbara Edlmair, Dr Mahnaz Emami, Salar Farzad, KT Forster, Jonathan Freeman, Helen Gale, Liz-Ann Gayle, Vishal Handa, Sara Haq, Laxmi Hariharan, Barry Harrison, David Head, Abigail Hunt, Hanadi Jabado, Matthew Johnson, Lydia Kan, Grace Kelly, Paul Kember, Bali Kochar, Soonu Kochar, Vinay Kulkarni, Francesca Lahiguera, Teresa Loy, Vari McLuskie, Charles McDermott, Bruce McFee, Karen Macmillan, Anna Marietta, Dr Naazi Marouf-Key, Andrew Marstrand, Dr Lee Mollins, Glenn Moore, Andrea Moretti-Adimari, Caroline Morgan, Julie Nazerali, Dr Laura Nelson, Safaa Nhairy, Oz O'Neill, Helen Osborne, Dr Caroline Palmy, Deepika Patel, Judy Piatkus, Margaret Purkiss, Stéphane Rambosson, Leya Reddy, Anita Rolls, Dr Norman Rosenthal, Joe Salem, James Scott, Anita Shah, Dan Scoular, Sunita Sehmi, Nagila Selmi, Jana Sharaf, Jo Sharp, Jonathan Smith, Dr John Spackman, Ivana Sretenovic, Andrei Stepanov, Jane Strachey, Mirela Sula, Kahéna Tlili-Fitzgerald, Nikhil Vadgama, Rahima Valji, Krish Vells, Dr Preema Vig, Andrea von Finckenstein, Hema Vyas, Becky Walsh, John Williams, Nick Williams, Roger Wilson, Susanne Worsfold and Ping Xu.

Further Information

Mindfulness

Right mindfulness is the seventh factor in the Noble Eightfold Path, which is the fourth of Buddha's four noble truths. There are many ways to learn mindfulness. One is the Headspace app designed by Andy Puddicombe, a former Buddhist monk. Thich Nhat Hanh's UK organisation is at www.coiuk.org.

Paramahamsa Nithyananda

Sri Nithyananda Swami was born in 1978. He runs free and paid-for programmes, both in person and via video link. His organisation has centres all over the world.
www.nithyananda.org.

Transcendental Meditation (TM)

TM is a form of mantra meditation which comes from the Vedic tradition. In the 1960s Maharishi Mahesh Yogi introduced TM to the West: www.tm.org. The Maharishi Foundation operates worldwide. The UK organisation is at www.uk.tm.org